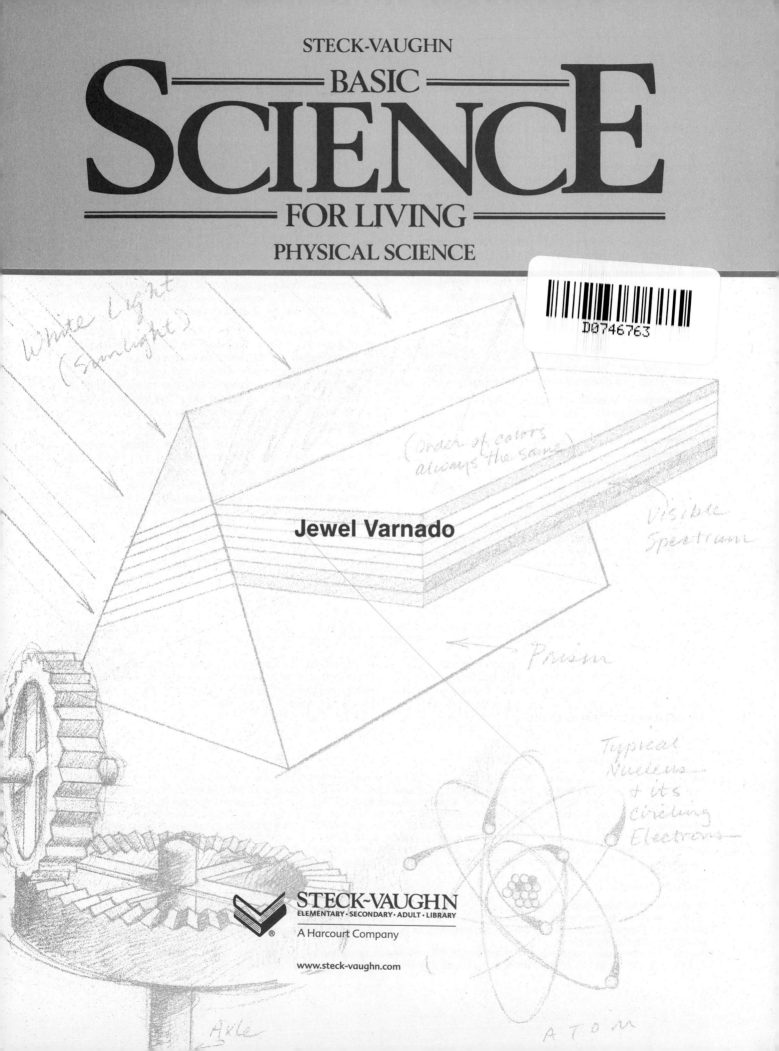

STECK-VAUGHN

BASIC
SCIENCE
FOR LIVING
PHYSICAL SCIENCE

Jewel Varnado

STECK-VAUGHN
ELEMENTARY · SECONDARY · ADULT · LIBRARY
A Harcourt Company

www.steck-vaughn.com

To the Teacher and the Student

Basic Science for Living is a two-book program specially designed for students who need to learn or review the basic scientific facts covered in a general science course. In *Earth and Life Science,* and *Physical Science,* students are introduced to science concepts through an explanation of the real-life science they experience every day. Students gain a thorough understanding of scientific terms and concepts from the relevant setting in which terms and concepts are presented. Mastering science is a challenging task. Special care has been taken in preparing both the organization and content of these books to guide the student to meeting this challenge with success.

- Each worktext is written in a manner that develops a high degree of reading comprehension and vocabulary, while providing a thorough survey of basic science. The author uses a conversational style of writing and consistent method of introducing, defining, and explaining scientific terms and processes to make the content lively, informative, and relevant for both student and teacher.

- Important science terms are highlighted and defined within the text. These terms are also defined and page referenced in a glossary at the back of each book.

- In each book, scientific facts and ideas have been grouped into seven units of related knowledge. *Earth and Life Science* begins with a discussion of the universe and our planet's place in the universe, then proceeds to discuss water, air, plants, animals, the human body, and health. *Physical Science* explores force and energy, thermal energy and heat, magnetism and electricity, light, sound, matter, and radioactivity and how these properties relate to our daily lives.

- Each unit is divided into several self-contained lessons. A review at the end of every lesson comprehensively tests the lesson's content. Lesson reviews follow five consistent, standardized formats that prepare students for other types of standardized assessment tools.

- Two black dots in the left margin of each lesson review signal critical thinking questions specially prepared to challenge students to apply knowledge they have gained to new situations.

- Each unit also presents two special features to make science more relevant to students lives. An *Issues in Science* lesson points out current science-related topics that are the subject of controversy or part of a trend in general science today. A *Careers* feature at the end of each unit points out careers in which general and/or specific science knowledge is important. Each career feature also provides a bibliography of books and associations for obtaining more information about careers in the area of science being discussed.

- A Mastery Review at the end of each book provides a chance to check mastery of important concepts and gives students practice with the commonly used separate-answer-sheet format. Clearly explained directions for the review allow it to be administered by the teacher or by students themselves.

- An easy-to-use Answer Key can be found at the back of each worktext. The answer key was prepared with both teacher and student use in mind. Students working independently will find the answer key an invaluable resource for checking their mastery of each lesson's concepts as presented in the lesson review. However, the answer key is perforated to allow easy removal for use in more traditional settings.

- The *Basic Science for Living* program was designed to bring science to students in a meaningful and useful way. The clarity of presentation, self-contained lessons, timely reviews, interesting features, glossary, mastery review, and answer key facilitate learning in a variety of educational situations—traditional classroom, small group seminar, tutorial instruction, and independent-study. The current and comprehensive content of *Basic Science for Living* provides students with the knowledge essential to understanding the world in which we live—a most exciting and interesting place.

About the Author

Jewel Varnado earned her bachelor's and master's degrees in educational psychology and her Ph.D. in adult education from Florida State University. She has received the Florida Adult Education Association's Outstanding Service Award and has successfully served as an instructor and a supervisor of adult education in Florida. She is the author of several children's books, a series of high-school English books *(English: Practice for Mastery),* and an English refresher course for adults *(English Essentials).*

Acknowledgments

Cover & Inside Illustrations (all but p. 22): Robert Priest

p. 4 © David Powers/Stock, Boston; **p. 11** HUD; **p. 14** Ford Motor Company; **p. 16** © Ellis Herwig/Stock, Boston; **p. 18** © Daniel S. Brody/Stock, Boston; **p. 24** Richard Hutchings; **p. 26** (both) Exxon Corporation; **p. 27** Southern California Edison Company; **p. 28** © Michael Hayman/Stock, Boston; **p. 30** International Brotherhood of Electrical Workers; **p. 32** National Weather Service; **p. 34** HUD; **p. 36** Tennessee Valley Authority; **p. 38** Sandy Wilson; **p. 40** © Daniel S. Brody/Stock, Boston; **p. 42** Courtesy of Con Edison; **p. 54** Westinghouse Electric Corporation; **p. 56** © Peter Simon/Stock, Boston; **p. 58** AT&T; **p. 60** © D. Aronson/Stock, Boston; **p. 66** AT&T; **p. 68** Courtesy of Con Edison; **p. 70** © Peter Menzel/Stock, Boston; **p. 72** Texico, Inc; **p. 76** © Ellis Herwig/Stock, Boston; **p. 82** Environmental Protection Agency; **p. 84** © Addison Geary/Stock, Boston; **p. 86** Duke Power Company; **p. 88** American Iron & Steel Institute; **p. 90** Oak Ridge National Laboratory; **p. 96** © Jean-Claude LeJeune/Stock, Boston.

ISBN 0-8114-4062-1

Contents

Unit One Force and Energy

Lesson 1 Energy   4–5
Lesson 2 Forces and Motion   6–7
Lesson 3 Machines   8–9
Lesson 4 The Usefulness of Machines 10–11
Lesson 5 Energy Transfer in an
          Automobile   12–13
Issues in Science—Robotics   14–15
Careers in Science   16–17

Unit Two Thermal Energy and Heat

Lesson 1 Thermal Energy and Heat   18–19
Lesson 2 Temperature   20–21
Lesson 3 Transferring Thermal Energy 22–23
Lesson 4 Home-Heating Systems   24–25
**Issues in Science—Solar-Heating
                    Systems**   26–27
Careers in Science   28–29

Unit Three Magnetism and Electricity

Lesson 1 Magnetism   30–31
Lesson 2 Matter and Electricity   32–33
Lesson 3 Current Electricity   34–35
Lesson 4 Using Electricity   36–37
Issues in Science—Electronics   38–39
Careers in Science   40–41

Unit Four Light

Lesson 1 The Electromagnetic
          Spectrum   42–43
Lesson 2 Light–Visible Radiation   44–45
Lesson 3 Reflection   46–47
Lesson 4 Refraction   48–49
Lesson 5 Color   50–51
Lesson 6 Other Properties of Light   52–53
Issues in Science—Lasers   54–55
Careers in Science   56–57

Unit Five Sound

Lesson 1 Sound   58–59
Lesson 2 Other Characteristics of
          Sound   60–61
Lesson 3 Noise and Music   62–63
Lesson 4 Acoustics   64–65
Lesson 5 Communicating with Sound 66–67
Issues in Science—Noise Pollution   68–69
Careers in Science   70–71

Unit Six Matter

Lesson 1 Matter   72–73
Lesson 2 Elements   74–75
Lesson 3 Chemical Reactions   76–77
Lesson 4 The Periodic Table   78–80
**Issues in Science—Environmental
                    Pollution**   81–83
Careers in Science   84–85

Unit Seven Radioactivity

Lesson 1 Radiation and Radioactivity 86–87
Lesson 2 Detecting Radioactivity   88–89
Lesson 3 Fission and Fusion   90–91
Lesson 4 Nuclear Reactors   92–93
Issues in Science—Nuclear Energy 94–95
Careers in Science   96–97

Glossary   98–103
Mastery Review   104–108
Answer Sheet   109
Answer Key   110–112
Mastery Review Answer Key   112

Force and Energy

Many machines change energy into work.

Energy

Scientists define **energy** as the ability to do work. An object has energy if it is able to produce a change in itself or in its surroundings. **Work** is the transfer of energy as the result of motion. If there is no motion, there is no work.

The **law of conservation of energy** states that the amount of energy in the universe is always the same. Energy cannot be created or destroyed. Energy can only be transferred, or changed, from one form into another. For example, energy transfer occurs when electrical energy is changed into radiant energy when a light bulb is switched on.

Everything has energy either because of its condition or position, or because of its motion. **Potential energy,** or stored energy, is energy available for use. There is potential energy in your muscles, in the string attached to a bow, in the gasoline in your car, and in a piece of coal. When potential energy is

converted into motion, it is called **kinetic energy.** Kinetic energy appears when you move your muscles, when the bow string vibrates, when your car moves, and when the piece of coal is burned.

The kinetic energy and potential energy in moving your muscles are forms of mechanical energy. Many machines change mechanical energy into work. The motor in a power lawn mower, for example, transfers the chemical energy in its fuel into mechanical energy that moves its parts. The movement of these parts allows the mower's blades to cut grass.

There are many forms of potential energy: chemical, electrical, radiant, magnetic, thermal, and nuclear. Chemical energy is found in foods and other forms of fuel. The stored energy in food and gasoline helps our bodies and cars to move. Electrical energy helps to run the appliances in our houses. Light is one form of radiant energy. Magnetic energy is used by an electric motor. Thermal energy, which is commonly and incorrectly referred to as heat, is the total energy of all the particles that make up a substance. **Heat** is the energy transferred from an object at a higher temperature to an object at a lower temperature. Nuclear energy is potential energy provided by the nucleus of an atom.

Energy is measured in different units. All of these units can be expressed in terms of the amount of work that is done. The work done to or by an object is the force multiplied by the distance over which the force acted or, more simply, force times distance equals work. A **force** is a push or a pull that one body or object exerts on another. If you move a one-pound box a distance of one foot, how much work did you do? By multiplying one pound by one foot, the amount of work done is one foot-pound. A foot-pound is the amount of work done when a one-pound object is moved a distance of one foot. ■

Lesson Review

On the line before each statement, write the letter of the choice that best completes the statement.

_____ 1. _____ is the ability to do work.

      a. Force   b. Energy   c. Power   d. Transfer

_____ 2. The transfer of energy as a result of motion is _____.

      a. force   b. power   c. work   d. physical

_____ 3. The law of conservation of energy states that _____.

      a. all energy comes from the sun   c. the amount of energy always changes

      b. energy can be created or destroyed   d. none of the above

_____ 4. Energy that is available for use is _____ energy.

      a. work   b. potential   c. kinetic   d. forceful

_____ 5. Energy of motion is also called _____ energy.

      a. work   b. potential   c. kinetic   d. forceful

_____ 6. Chemical energy is a kind of _____ energy.

      a. potential   b. kinetic   c. radiant   d. mechanical

_____ 7. _____ energy is used by an electric motor to do work.

      a. Chemical   b. Magnetic   c. Nuclear   d. Thermal

_____ 8. The energy transferred from an object at a higher temperature to one at a lower temperature is _____.

      a. thermal energy   b. radiant energy   c. magnetic energy   d. heat

● _____ 9. Which of the following is an example of kinetic energy?

      a. a person jogging   b. an operating fan   c. a moving train   d. all of the above

● _____ 10. _____ is <u>not</u> an example of work being done.

      a. A person lifting an object   c. A dog carrying a bone

      b. A person winding a clock   d. A person pushing against a wall

Forces and Motion

Recall that work is done to an object or by an object only if there is movement or motion. What is motion? **Motion** can be defined as a change in position. Earth rotating on its axis, the movement of a second hand on a clock, and a car slowing down at a stop sign are all examples of objects in motion.

How fast is Earth rotating on its axis? How fast is the clock hand moving? How slow is the car going? **Speed** is the rate of change of the position of an object. Speed is measured in units of distance covered in a set amount of time. Earth rotates on its axis at a speed of about 330 miles per hour. The second hand on a clock moves one position every second. A car slowing down at a stop sign may be moving at a speed of less than ten miles per hour.

Velocity refers to an object's speed and the direction in which it is moving. Velocity is measured in units of distance and time. Velocity changes if either the speed of the object or the direction of the object changes. For example, two airplanes may be traveling at 600 miles per hour, but if one is traveling east and the other is headed west, they have different velocities.

When the velocity of an object changes, the object is either accelerating or decelerating. If the velocity increases, the object is accelerating. If the velocity decreases, as is the case with the car slowing down at a stop sign, the object is decelerating. **Acceleration** is the increased rate of change in an object's velocity. **Deceleration** is the decreased rate of change in an object's velocity. In other words, acceleration and deceleration are measures of the change in velocity of an object over a certain period of time. The acceleration of an object is calculated by subtracting the initial velocity from the final velocity and dividing that number by the time over which the change occurred. The units used to measure acceleration are a distance covered in an amount of time multiplied by time.

Suppose a car moves westward at 30 miles per hour. What is its velocity? The velocity of the car is 30 miles per hour to the west. Now suppose the car increases its velocity to 40 miles per hour, in one minute. The acceleration of the car is equal to 40 miles per hour minus 30 miles per hour divided by one minute. The acceleration, then, is 10 miles an hour in one minute toward the west.

Isaac Newton, a famous seventeenth century scientist, was one of the first people to study and understand motion. He developed three scientific laws to explain motion. Newton's **first law of motion** states that an object moving at a constant velocity will continue at that velocity unless acted upon by an outside force. The law also states that an object at rest will tend to remain at rest unless acted upon by an outside force.

Newton's first law is sometimes called the law of inertia. **Inertia** is a property of an object that resists any change in velocity. In order to change the velocity of an object, inertia must be overcome. If you have ever tried to push a stalled car with an automatic transmission, you probably found that it takes a great amount of force to get the car moving. Once the car is in motion, however, the effort to keep it in motion is less than the initial effort. To stop the car again, however, requires a large effort; inertia is acting to keep the car moving. The amount of mass an object has is a measure of its inertia. **Mass** is the amount of matter that makes up an object.

What happens if an outside force acts upon an object? Newton's **second law of motion** states that the acceleration of an object increases as the amount of the force applied on the object increases. The force applied is equal to the object's mass multiplied by the acceleration. The greater the mass of an object, the slower the acceleration. The greater the force applied, the greater the acceleration.

Newton's **third law of motion** states that forces always come in pairs. Therefore, for every action, there is an opposite and equal reaction. You probably didn't realize that if you stand on a carpeted floor and push against a wall, the wall is pushing back against you with equal force. That is why neither you nor the wall moves.

You may be aware of some of the forces that affect your motion. You know, for example, that it is easier to slide on ice than it is to slide across a carpeted floor. **Friction** is a force that opposes or counteracts the motion between two surfaces that are in contact. Which surface provides more friction—the ice or the carpet?

Why does an object fall to the ground when it is dropped? The force of **gravity** pulls objects toward Earth. Gravity exists among all objects. The greater the mass of an object, the greater the force of gravity it exerts. The force of gravity also depends on the distance between two objects. The farther two objects are away from one another, the less the gravitational force is between them. The force of gravity that Earth exerts on an object at its surface is called the object's **weight.** ■

Lesson Review

In the space provided, write the word or words that best complete the statement.

1. _____ is a change in position.

2. The rate of change of position is called _____.

3. A fielder catching a fly ball is an example of Newton's _____ law of motion.

4. _____ is a property of an object that resists any change in velocity.

5. The amount of matter that makes up an object is the object's _____.

6. According to Newton's second law of motion, pulling a sled with one rider requires _____ force than pulling a sled with three passengers.

7. Newton's third law of motion states that forces always come in _____.

8. A carpeted surface provides _____ friction than a sheet of ice.

● 9. A runner runs west at a speed of two miles an hour on a straight road. She turns left and continues at two miles an hour. The runner's _____ has changed.

● 10. As the mass of an object increases, so does its weight. When you diet, you lose mass. Therefore, your weight _____.

What do a car engine, a hammer, a screw, a doorknob, and a printing press have in common? All are machines. A **machine** is a device that does work by changing one form of energy into another form of energy in order to create force. To do work, a machine changes the speed, the amount, or the direction of a force in order to produce motion.

There are many kinds of machines. Some are very complex, such as a printing press. Crowbars and hammers, on the other hand, are simple machines. Scientists define a simple machine as a machine that is made of only one part. There are six simple machines: the lever, the wheel and axle, the pulley, the inclined plane, the wedge, and the screw.

A **lever** is a simple machine consisting of a bar or rod that turns about a supporting point called a **fulcrum.** Look at the illustration. The man is using a lever made of a wooden pole and a log to move the rock. Notice that one end of the pole is under the rock. The log is the fulcrum. By applying a downward force on the pole, the man can move the rock. If he moved the fulcrum closer to the rock, would it be easier or harder for him to move it?

The weight of an object moved by a machine is its **resistance**. The force used to move the object is the **effort.** In a lever, the distance from the resistance to the fulcrum is called the resistance arm. The distance from the fulcrum to the effort is the effort arm. The resistance multiplied by the resistance arm is always equal to the effort times the effort arm. The work put out by a machine never exceeds the amount of work put into the machine.

Look again at the illustration. Suppose the rock weighs 75 pounds. The length of the pole is five feet, and the log is two feet from the rock. What amount of force is needed to move the rock? The resistance, 75 pounds, multiplied by its resistance arm, two feet, equals 150 foot-pounds. The effort times the effort arm, three feet, also must equal 150 foot-pounds. Therefore, the minimum effort needed to move the rock is 150 foot-pounds divided by three feet, or 50 pounds. If the fulcrum is placed one foot from the rock, would the needed effort be more or less than 50 pounds?

Construction tools, such as power shovels, cranes, and other loading equipment, use levers to do work. Some of these tools use a special form of a lever called a wheel and axle. A **wheel and axle** is a simple machine that consists of a large wheel that is attached to a smaller wheel or rod called an axle. You have seen a wheel and axle at work when using a doorknob or a pencil sharpener.

A **pulley** is a simple machine in which a rope or cable is strung over a grooved wheel. A pulley changes the direction of the effort. A **block and tackle** is a combination of two or more pulleys which can be used to lift heavy equipment. Construction workers and window washers often use pulleys to raise and lower themselves along the sides of buildings.

An **inclined plane** is simply a slanted surface. Inclined planes are often used by people moving furniture or other heavy objects. It is nearly impossible for a person to lift a 300-pound object from the ground into the back of a truck. But if a plank is placed from the truck to the ground, it takes much less effort to get the object into the truck.

A wedge is a special kind of inclined plane. A **wedge** is an inclined plane that has either one or two slanted edges. Wedges include the sharp ends of knives and most other cutting tools, axes, plows, and chisels.

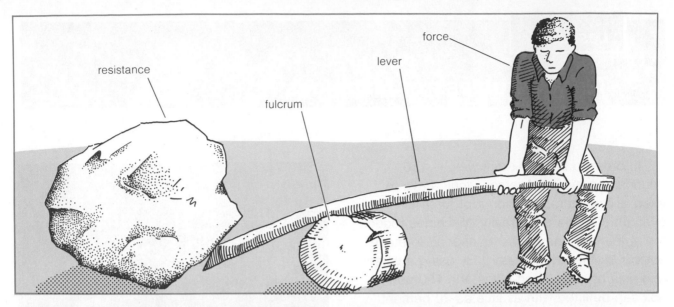

A lever is a machine that may be used to change the amount and direction of force needed to do work.

A **screw** is really an inclined plane wrapped around a shaft or cylinder. If you look at a screw from the side, you will notice that its threads spiral upward. There are many different kinds of screws. Wood screws are used in pieces of furniture. Metal screws are found in many machine parts. Large screws called jack screws can lift cars and houses.

Many of the machines you use are combinations of simple machines. A bicycle is a combination of levers and wheels and axles. A machine made of two or more simple machines is called a **compound machine.** ∎

Lesson Review

In the space before each number, write the letter of the word or group of words in Column 2 that matches the description in Column 1.

Column 1	Column 2
_____ 1. the supporting point of a lever	a. compound machine
_____ 2. the weight of an object being moved by a machine	b. effort
_____ 3. the force used to move an object	c. fulcrum
_____ 4. a simple machine made of a rope and a wheel	d. inclined plane
_____ 5. an inclined plane with one or two slanted edges	e. lever
_____ 6. an inclined plane wrapped around a shaft	f. pulley
_____ 7. a combination of two or more simple machines	g. resistance
_____ 8. a compound machine made of a lever and wedge	h. screw
● _____ 9. a ramp is this type of simple machine	i. shovel
● _____ 10. a hand-held bottle opener is this type of simple machine	j. wedge

9

The Usefulness of Machines

In order to lift a box that weighs 150 pounds, the average person would have to exert a considerable amount of force to overcome inertia and gravity. Machines reduce the amount of energy that is needed to move objects that are quite heavy. By using a wheel and axle or an inclined plane, the 150-pound box can be lifted with as little as 20 percent of the force that would be needed if the box were lifted by hand.

The usefulness of a machine can be described using three terms: mechanical advantage, efficiency, and power. **Mechanical advantage** is the number of times that the effort is multiplied by using the machine to move the resistance. Recall that the effort is the force that is needed to move an object. The weight of an object is its resistance. If a machine uses four pounds of force to move a 20-pound object, what is the machine's mechanical advantage? By dividing the weight of the object by the amount of force needed to move it, the mechanical advantage is found. The mechanical advantage of the machine is five.

What is the relationship between mechanical advantage and energy? The greater the mechanical advantage of a machine, the less energy that is needed to do a job. A block and tackle has a high mechanical advantage. Would these machines be better for lifting lightweight objects or very heavy objects?

Recall that the law of conservation of energy states that energy can neither be created nor destroyed. As a result, no more energy can be gotten out of a machine than the amount of energy that is put into it. The work that a machine does is the machine's **output.** The output is the amount of energy released by the machine when doing a job. The energy that is put or designed into a machine is the

Simple machines, such as pulleys, have high efficiencies.

machine's **input.** The machine's input is the amount of energy that a machine has available to release in order to get the job done. The output of a machine is always less than its input because of the action of gravity, inertia, and friction.

The **efficiency** of a machine is the relationship between the force it puts out and the force that it could put out if it did not have to overcome the forces of gravity, inertia, and friction that are acting upon it. A machine's efficiency is expressed as a percentage, with 100 percent being perfect efficiency. Of course, no machine has 100 percent efficiency due to the energy lost in overcoming friction.

A simple machine, such as a crowbar, approaches 100 percent efficiency because it must overcome very little friction. Many compound machines, on the other hand, have low efficiencies. Most automobile engines, for example, are only about 25 percent efficient. About 75 percent of the chemical energy released by gasoline is used to overcome the friction that is developed by the many moving parts of the engine. To improve the efficiency of many machines, smoother surfaces, ball bearings, and a variety of lubricants are used to help reduce friction. Reducing friction makes the machines more efficient and cheaper to operate.

Power is the rate at which a machine does work. In other words, power is the amount of work done in a certain amount of time. The greater the power of a machine, the faster it completes a job. It takes more power to do work in five minutes than it does to do the same work in ten minutes.

The power of most mechanical machines is measured in foot-pounds per second. Recall that one foot-pound is the amount of work done when moving a one-pound object a distance of one foot. Horsepower was originally used to represent the amount of power that an average horse could deliver. The term is now used to measure the power delivered by many engines and motors. One horsepower equals 550 foot-pounds of work completed in one second. ■

Lesson Review

In the space provided, write the word or words that best complete the statement.

1. To lift a box, a machine has to overcome the forces of _____ and _____.

2. _____ is the number of times the effort is multiplied in moving the resistance.

3. The greater the mechanical advantage of a machine, the _____ energy needed to do the job.

4. The _____ of a machine is the work that the machine does.

5. _____ is the relationship between a machine's input and output.

6. Compound machines have _____ efficiencies.

7. Reducing _____ makes machines more efficient and therefore cheaper to operate.

8. The rate at which a machine does a job is the _____ of the machine.

● 9. A machine that puts out five pounds of force to move a 30-pound object has a mechanical advantage of _____.

● 10. A machine such as a lever has a very _____ mechanical advantage.

Energy Transfer in an Automobile

An automobile is a compound machine. Recall that a compound machine is a machine made of two or more simple machines. An automobile is made of many simple machines. Most people get into a car, put the key into the ignition, start it up, and drive away. Many of them don't realize that energy is being transferred many times as the car does work. How does your car work?

Recall that chemical energy is stored in gasoline. In order for the car's engine to do work, this chemical energy must be released and transferred to the various other parts of the car so that the car will do what it was designed to do. A crankshaft, which is really the simple machine called a wheel and axle, is set into motion when energy from the burning fuel causes the shaft to turn. This shaft is connected to the engine's pistons. As the shaft turns, the pistons move up and down. The revolving shaft also transfers energy to a flywheel, which is attached to the rear of the engine. The flywheel transfers energy to the car's transmission.

An automobile's transmission is a system of gears. **Gears** are wheels with teeth, or notches, around their outer edges. The notches of two gears fit together to keep the gears from slipping as they turn, and allow the gears to work smoothly as they transfer energy.

The transmission in most cars consists of four forward gears and one reverse gear. When you drive a car with a standard transmission, you are able to select the proper gear needed to produce the speed that you need in a particular situation. Low, or first, gear provides the maximum force and slow speed needed to move the car or to drive up steep hills. Second gear produces less force and more speed than first gear. Third and fourth gears are used for faster driving.

Do these gears provide more or less force than second gear? Why?

Gears transfer energy to the car's drive shaft. The **drive shaft** is a rod that runs from the transmission to the car's rear axle. At the rear axle, the rotating drive shaft transfers energy to another set of gears called the **differential,** which is mounted to the center of the rear axle.

The differential is made of several simple machines. Recall that any machine changes the speed, the amount of force, or the direction of force in order to do work. When your car makes a right turn, the left rear wheel travels farther and faster than the right rear wheel. It is the differential that allows the two rear wheels to turn at different rates. Look at the illustration. What other purpose does the differential serve? The differential also changes the direction of the force from the drive shaft to the rear wheels and axle.

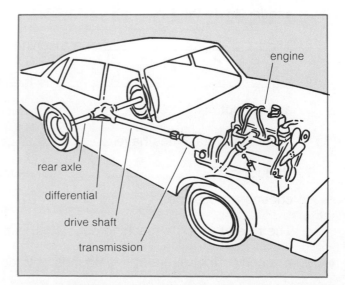

Energy is transferred from a car's engine down the drive shaft to the rear wheels.

A gear at the end of the drive shaft meshes with gears on each end of the rear axle. The rear axle is connected to each of the back wheels of the car. This final transfer of energy allows the wheels of the car to turn. If the car is a front-wheel drive model, energy is channeled in a similar way to the car's front wheels, rather than to the rear wheels.

Recall that friction is a force that must be overcome in order for machines to do work. Recall also that most automobile engines are only about 25 percent efficient. To improve your car's efficiency, friction must be reduced. To combat friction, lubrication is essential to the maintenance of any compound machine, including your car. Oil and grease are two lubricants used to reduce friction in automobiles. Oil in the engine's crankcase lubricates the pistons and the drive shaft. Fluid in the transmission lubricates its gears. Grease is used to reduce friction produced by the meshing gears in the differential. Belts and other moving parts also require special lubrication in order to operate smoothly. ■

Lesson Review

In the space before each number, write the letter of the word or group of words in Column 2 that matches the description in Column 1.

Column 1

_____ 1. shaft that is set into motion from the burning of gasoline

_____ 2. car part that transfers energy to the car's transmission

_____ 3. wheels with teeth or notches around their outer edges

_____ 4. shaft that runs from the transmission to the rear axle

_____ 5. allows the rear wheels of a car to travel at different speeds

_____ 6. rod connected to both rear wheels

_____ 7. force that must be overcome in order for a machine to do work

_____ 8. reduces friction in the drive shaft and in the engine's pistons

● _____ 9. reduces friction in automobile wheels

● _____ 10. energy source for an automobile engine

Column 2

a. ball bearings

b. crankshaft

c. differential

d. drive shaft

e. flywheel

f. friction

g. gasoline

h. gears

i. oil

j. rear axle

Robotics

Most people are probably first introduced to robots in a work of science fiction. In science fiction films and television series, robots are usually pictured as humanlike machines that can walk and talk. However, robots used in industry today have very little in common with those shown in science fiction books or movies. Today's **robot** is a machine that usually remains in a fixed position and is guided by a computer to complete a task. Designs differ and are changed rapidly, but most robots have single arms that lift objects and use tools.

The science and technology of designing and using robots to do work is called **robotics.** Robots can do work that is too boring, difficult, or dangerous for humans. Robots, for example, are often used to do welding on automobile assembly lines. Many people find this to be boring work when it is done for long periods of time. Robots also do some kinds of intense physical labor in mining and agriculture that can be too difficult for people to do. Some robots work in steel mills and nuclear power plants where certain tasks are too dangerous for human beings.

For a robot to work effectively, it must be controlled by a computer. The computer guides the robot with instructions that lead the machine through the steps of a job. The computer is also programmed to monitor the robot's work. If the robot is not performing as it should, the computer makes adjustments or shuts down the robot for maintenance or repairs.

The process that makes it possible to regulate a machine such as a robot with a computer is called feedback. **Feedback** allows the robot to "tell" the computer how the robot is operating and what its surroundings are like. To make feedback possible, the robot is fitted with a sensor. A **sensor** is a device, such as an electric eye, a camera, or a microchip, which transmits information about the robot's performance and surroundings to the computer. The computer then makes adjustments to the robot when necessary. Without feedback, a robot is only a machine that does the same task over and over again.

For example, by using feedback, a robot can work on an assembly line where five or six different kinds of products have to be welded. The robot's sensors send information about the approaching product to the computer. The computer adjusts the robot to weld that product. When a different product rolls down the assembly line, the computer readjusts the robot to weld that particular product. In fact, today, robots are used more in welding than in any other industrial operation.

Robots are used in other industrial operations, as well. Some robots handle heavy materials that are needed in manufacturing. Items weighing up to 2,000 pounds can be easily lifted and stacked by certain kinds of robots! Robots are also commonly used to apply spray finishes and other protective

An automatic welding robot encloses a car body and makes about 70 spot welds a minute.

coatings to a variety of products. Inhaling the fumes from the coatings can be hazardous to humans but do no harm to robots. Robots are also able to perform a variety of machining operations, including cutting, grinding, drilling, polishing, and sanding.

Robots are just beginning to be used in the kinds of product assembly that demand fine adjustments. Robots have been designed to fit together screws, nuts, bolts, and other fastening devices. Certain robots are able to inspect finished products. Equipped with special visual systems, these machines are able to make difficult but necessary quality control checks on a variety of products.

The development of the microchip has made it possible to create robots that can work efficiently and effectively. Much, however, remains to be done. Robots that can move themselves more effortlessly from place to place are yet to be designed. Devices have not been developed that will give robotic machines handling capabilities near the abilities of human hands. Robots equipped with sensors that function in ways similar to human eyes and ears are a long way from perfection. Experts in robotics, however, believe that such machines can be built and used to improve our lives in the future. ■

Lesson Review

In the space provided, write the word or words that best complete the statement.

1. In industry today, a robot is a stationary machine that is guided by

   a(n) _____.

2. _____ is the science of designing and using robots to do work.

3. Robots perform tasks that are too dangerous, boring, or _____

   for humans.

4. _____ is the process that allows a robot to communicate with its

   computer.

5. Today, robots are used more in _____ than in any other

   industrial operation.

6. Cameras, electric eyes, and microchips are robot _____.

7. Spray finishes that are _____ to humans can be applied by robots

   with no problems.

8. Fitting together screws, nuts, bolts, and other fastening devices are fine

   _____ that some robots are able to do.

● 9. Initially, robots were very large; _____ have made it possible to make

   smaller robots.

● 10. In a soft drink bottling plant, a specially designed robot might use its

   _____ system to determine whether or not bottles are properly filled.

Petroleum engineers supervise the building of drilling rigs and oversee the operation of refineries.

Petroleum engineers supervise the building of the drilling rigs that are set up in places where oil is likely to be found. They see to it that proper equipment and methods are used in the drilling process. Once oil is found, petroleum engineers oversee the operation of the well. They make sure that pumps are properly operated and maintained so that oil flows smoothly through pipelines and into storage tanks. Petroleum engineers also check on the quality of the oil and keep track of the amounts that are taken from a well. Petroleum engineers work for petroleum companies and for companies that specialize in the location of petroleum reserves.

Mechanical engineers work with a wide variety of machines and tools that transfer energy. Often working as part of a team that includes scientists and technicians, mechanical engineers help to develop engines, elevators, printing presses, drill presses, bulldozers, and numerous other machines and devices. They work on tiny mechanisms and huge gears. Most mechanical engineers work for manufacturing companies.

Safety engineers design structures and equipment to make people's jobs as safe as possible. Safety engineers are commonly employed in the mining industry. They inspect the working area carefully to be sure that the danger from falling rocks is small. Safety engineers are also concerned with proper ventilation and the presence of dangerous gases in the mine shaft. Some safety engineers work for federal agencies, such as the Mine Safety and Health Administration.

Automobile mechanics often begin their careers by working under the direction of an experienced mechanic in a garage, service station, or automobile dealership. Those who work in a dealership often obtain advanced training from the auto manufacturers' technical specialists. Some mechanics specialize in the service and repair of a certain system of an automobile. Many mechanics work for companies that operate several repair facilities. Some own and manage their own businesses.

Construction workers use heavy machinery to build roads, highways, and other projects. These workers sometimes begin as helpers to heavy equipment operators. Many construction workers, however, obtain training in heavy equipment operation at private trade schools or in training programs managed by construction unions. Most construction workers work for private contractors. Some work for local and state highway departments.

In the energy field, opportunities are available to those with some technical background. Petroleum and mining companies employ various types of engineering and laboratory technicians. Industries that use the sun to produce other forms of energy employ architectural technicians. Jobs are also available for those who work directly with petroleum engineers and geologists in the fossil fuels industries. Solar energy companies employ sheet metal workers and installers, among other workers. ∎

For Further Information

More information about these and related careers is available from the following publications and organizations.

What's It Like to Be an Engineer?, General Electric Company, 1982

Engineering: The Career and the Profession, W. Edward Red, Brooks Cole, 1982

Accreditation Board for Engineering and Technology
345 East 47th Street
New York, NY 10017

National Society of Professional Engineers
1420 King Street
Alexandria, VA 22314

Thermal Energy and Heat

This power plant changes chemical energy in fuel into radiant energy.

Lesson 1

Thermal Energy and Heat

A person sitting still, a boat at dock, and a fish lingering on the bottom of an aquarium are examples of energy due to an object's condition. Recall that this form of energy is called potential, or stored, energy. People walking, boats sailing, and fish swimming are examples of kinetic energy. Kinetic energy is the energy of motion.

People, boats, fish, and all other matter is made of tiny particles called molecules. Molecules are constantly moving. This movement is thermal energy. **Thermal energy** is the total energy, both kinetic and potential, of all the molecules that make up a substance.

The thermal energy of an object depends upon three factors: its mass, the type of matter it is made of, and its temperature. An object with more mass has more thermal energy than an object with less mass. A person has more thermal energy than a goldfish. A train, in turn, has more thermal energy than a person.

Different kinds of molecules make up different kinds of matter. The molecules that make up people, for example, are different from the molecules that make up fish. The molecules in people move at different rates from the molecules in fish. The more rapidly the molecules that make up an object move, the more thermal energy the object has. Steam and water are made of the same kind of molecules. Steam molecules move faster than the molecules of water. A set mass of steam has more thermal energy than the same mass of water.

Thermal energy is also related to temperature. **Temperature** is a measure of the average kinetic energy of the particles that make up an object. In other words, temperature is a measure of the movement of the particles in an object. Objects with higher temperatures have greater thermal energies. For example, a certain mass of water has more energy than ice with the same mass. The molecules in water move faster than the molecules in ice.

Energy cannot be created or destroyed. Energy is transferred from one object to another. Heat is thermal energy that is transferred from an object at a higher temperature to an object at a lower temperature. A campfire provides heat as the chemical energy stored in wood is changed into radiant energy. The sun heats our planet as its thermal energy is transferred to Earth as radiant energy. If

you hold a cup of hot coffee, you can feel the heat that flows from the hot cup to your hand.

You have just learned that heat flows from an object with a higher temperature to an object with a lower temperature. But what happens to the heat from warm food when it is put in the refrigerator? The refrigerator cools the food. The thermal energy is transferred from the food to the refrigerator. The refrigerator, in turn, transfers the heat to the kitchen. ■

Lesson Review

Fill in the circle containing the letter of the term or phrase that correctly completes each statement.

1. Stored energy is also called _____ energy.
   - ⓐ kinetic
   - ⓑ temperature
   - ⓒ potential
   - ⓓ heat

2. _____ energy is the energy of movement.
   - ⓐ Kinetic
   - ⓑ Temperature
   - ⓒ Potential
   - ⓓ Heat

3. All matter is made of _____.
   - ⓐ steam
   - ⓑ energy
   - ⓒ molecules
   - ⓓ all of the above

4. The total energy of all particles that make up an object is called _____.
   - ⓐ temperature
   - ⓑ thermal energy
   - ⓒ heat energy
   - ⓓ radiant energy

5. Thermal energy depends upon _____.
   - ⓐ the mass of an object
   - ⓑ the type of matter in the object
   - ⓒ the temperature of an object
   - ⓓ all of the above

6. _____ is a measure of the average kinetic energy of the particles that make up an object.
   - ⓐ Heat
   - ⓑ Potential
   - ⓓ Kinetic
   - ⓓ Temperature

7. Objects with _____ temperatures have higher thermal energies.
   - ⓐ freezing
   - ⓑ lower
   - ⓒ higher
   - ⓓ no

8. The thermal energy transferred from an object at a higher temperature to an object at a lower temperature is _____.
   - ⓐ molecular energy
   - ⓑ heat
   - ⓒ potential energy
   - ⓓ none of the above

● 9. A rowboat has more thermal energy than a(n) _____.
   - ⓐ large ship
   - ⓑ freight train
   - ⓒ elephant
   - ⓓ goldfish

● 10. A refrigerator _____ objects placed inside it.
   - ⓐ adds heat to
   - ⓑ removes heat from
   - ⓒ does not change the thermal energy of
   - ⓓ speeds up the molecules in

Temperature

All objects are made of tiny, constantly moving molecules. Thermal energy is the total energy of the molecules that make up an object. Temperature is a measure of the average kinetic energy of these molecules.

Why do your hands become warm when they are held over a campfire? Why does an iron pan heated on a stove become too hot to touch? Heat is the transfer of thermal energy from an object at a higher temperature to an object at a lower temperature. When the molecules that make up an object are heated, they gain energy. This increase in energy makes the molecules move faster. The increased movement causes a rise in the temperature.

Temperature is measured with a **thermometer**. Most thermometers are hollow tubes closed at both ends. Thermometers are partially filled with mercury or colored alcohol. How does a thermometer work? If a mercury thermometer is placed into a pail of water, the molecules of the thermometer bump into the molecules of water. Energy is transferred among the molecules of water and the molecules of the thermometer and the mercury inside. If the water is warmer than the mercury, the mercury in the thermometer expands, or spreads out, moving up the glass tube. If the water is colder than the mercury in the thermometer, the mercury contracts, or gets smaller, moving down the glass tube. When the average kinetic energy of the water equals that of the mercury, the movement of the water and mercury molecules is the same. Now the temperatures of the water and mercury are equal. The water temperature then can be read from the thermometer.

Temperature is measured in degrees. There are two scales used to measure

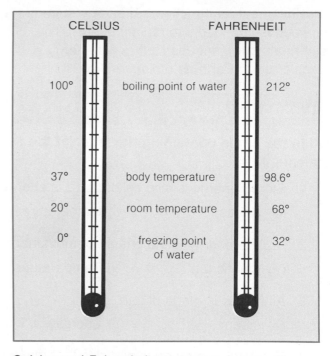

Celsius and Fahrenheit are two scales used to measure temperature.

temperature. The **Fahrenheit scale,** abbreviated by the letter *F,* is used by most people in the United States and Canada. The **Celsius scale,** which is based on the freezing and boiling points of water, is used by most countries of the world and by nearly all scientists. The Celsius scale is abbreviated by the letter *C.*

Water freezes at 32°F and boils at 212°F. Knowing this, you can find the freezing and boiling points of water on the Celsius scale. Degrees Fahrenheit can be converted to degrees Celsius by subtracting 32 degrees from the Fahrenheit reading and multiplying that number by $\frac{5}{9}$. The equation for this conversion is:

$$(°F - 32°) \times \frac{5}{9} = °C$$

To calculate the freezing point of water on the Celsius scale, subtract 32° from 32°F, the

Fahrenheit freezing point of water. Multiply this number by $\frac{5}{9}$. Zero times $\frac{5}{9}$ equals zero. The freezing point of water is 0°C. What is the boiling point of water in degrees Celsius?

Degrees Celsius can be changed to degrees Fahrenheit by multiplying the Celsius reading by $\frac{9}{5}$ and adding this number to 32°. The equation for converting degrees Celsius into degrees Fahrenheit is:

$$(°C \times \tfrac{9}{5}) + 32° = °F$$

What is the Fahrenheit equivalent of 50°C? ■

Lesson Review

On the line before each statement, write the letter of the choice that best completes the statement.

_____ 1. All objects are made of very tiny particles called _____.

    a. kinetics   b. heat   c. molecules   d. energies

_____ 2. _____ is the transfer of thermal energy from an object at a higher temperature to an object at a lower temperature.

    a. Heat   c. Temperature

    b. Thermometer   d. None of the above

_____ 3. Temperature is measured with an instrument called a(n) _____.

    a. energizer   b. Celsius   c. thermometer   d. Fahrenheit

_____ 4. If a substance is warmer than the mercury in a thermometer, the mercury will _____.

    a. contract   b. expand   c. fall   d. stay the same

_____ 5. Temperature is measured in _____.

    a. scales   b. energy   c. degrees   d. alcohol

_____ 6. The _____ scale is used to measure temperature by most people in the United States.

    a. Celsius   b. Fahrenheit   c. Kinetic   d. Energy

_____ 7. Zero degrees Celsius is equal to _____ degrees Fahrenheit.

    a. 3   b. 32   c. 150   d. 212

_____ 8. Degrees Celsius can be changed to degrees Fahrenheit by using which of the following equations?

    a. $(°C \times \tfrac{9}{5}) - 32° = °F$ c. $(°C \times \tfrac{9}{5}) + 32° = °F$

    b. $(°F - 32°) \times \tfrac{9}{5} = °C$ d. none of the above

● _____ 9. Water turns to ice at _____ °F.

    a. 0   b. 32   c. 37   d. 98.6

● _____ 10. The boiling point of water in degrees Celsius is _____.

    a. 32   b. 98.6   c. 100   d. 212

Transferring Thermal Energy

Thermal energy can be transferred in three ways: conduction, convection, and radiation. **Conduction** is the transfer of thermal energy that takes place when two objects at different temperatures are in contact with one another. For example, if one end of an iron rod is held in a flame, that end of the rod may become red hot. If the rod is left in the flame long enough, the opposite end of the rod may become too hot to hold.

How is thermal energy transferred from the flame along the iron rod? Thermal energy from the flame is absorbed by the molecules in the end of the iron rod that is in the flame. The increase in thermal energy increases the speed at which the iron molecules vibrate, or move back and forth. The faster moving molecules of the rod bump into nearby, cooler, slower moving molecules in the rod. Energy is transferred to the slower moving molecules, which, in turn, vibrate faster and bump into other nearby molecules. This process of conduction goes on down the rod until the energy of all the rod's molecules has increased. The increase in the energy of the molecules causes a rise in the temperature of the iron rod.

Conduction varies among different substances. The transfer of thermal energy by conduction is better in solids than in liquids or gases. Why? The molecules that make up solids are closer together than the molecules in either liquids or gases. **Conductors** are materials that transfer thermal energy. Some materials conduct heat better than others. Metals, for example, are good thermal conductors. Glass and plastics are not.

Although molecules bump into one another during conduction, the particles vibrate in relatively fixed positions. During **convection**, however, thermal energy is transferred by the actual movement of molecules. For example,

when a teapot containing water is heated, thermal energy is conducted from the stove burner to the bottom of the pot. Then, as the water in the bottom of the pot gets warmer, it becomes less dense and rises. The more dense cool water from the top of the pot sinks to replace the warmer water. This circular movement of water molecules is a convection current. Liquids and gases transfer thermal energy by convection.

You can observe a convection current by holding your hand above a lighted electric lamp. The air molecules near the lamp are warmed by the heat from the lamp. Since warm air rises, these warm-air molecules actually flow upward and carry heat from the lamp to your hand.

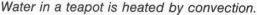

Water in a teapot is heated by convection.

When you hold your hand below the lighted lamp, do you feel heat? How does the heat travel down from the electric lamp? Since your hand is below the lamp, heat does not travel by convection. Convection currents only carry heat upward. Since your hand is not touching the lamp, the heat cannot travel by conduction. Conduction requires contact between molecules. Heat from the lamp is transmitted to your hand by radiation.

Radiation is the transfer of thermal energy that can take place in a vacuum. All objects, even people, give off radiant energy. You may have noticed that a room full of people is much warmer than an empty room. The energy emitted by the people is absorbed by the air in the room. Therefore, the room becomes warm. Radiant energy from the sun warms our planet. The light bulb from a lighted lamp emits radiant energy and warms the area below it. Radiant energy travels at a speed of 186,000 miles per second!

Radiant energy becomes thermal energy only when it strikes an object and is absorbed by the object. Radiant energy is not always absorbed. It may pass through an object, or it may be reflected away from the object. Radiant energy passes through transparent materials such as glass. It is absorbed by dark-colored materials. Shiny substances and light-colored materials usually reflect most of the radiant energy that reaches them. ■

Lesson Review

Determine whether each of the following statements is true or false. Correct each false statement by crossing out the word or phrase that makes it false and writing the correct word or phrase above it.

_____ 1. Thermal energy is transferred by conduction, convection, and radiation.

_____ 2. Convection is the transfer of energy that occurs when two objects at different temperatures are in contact with one another.

_____ 3. During conduction, an increase in thermal energy causes a decrease in the speed at which the molecules vibrate.

_____ 4. Conduction of thermal energy is better in solids than in liquids or gases.

_____ 5. Convection is the transfer of thermal energy by actual movement of molecules.

_____ 6. Cool water is less dense than warm water.

_____ 7. Liquids and gases transfer thermal energy by convection.

_____ 8. Convection is the transfer of energy that can take place in a vacuum.

• _____ 9. White clothing usually stays cooler than dark-colored clothing.

• _____ 10. To evenly heat a room by convection, you would place the incoming hot air register near the ceiling.

Home-Heating Systems

Before the nineteenth century, an open fireplace was the most common home-heating device. Thermal energy from the fire was transferred primarily by radiation and, to a lesser extent, by convection. Unfortunately, the convection currents that carried the smoke up to the chimney also carried away large amounts of heat. Clearly, a more efficient heating device was needed.

Pot-bellied iron stoves that burned wood or coal were the first home-heating devices designed to replace the fireplace. Although smoke from the fire still went up the chimney, much less heat escaped with it. How did these stoves heat a room?

Thermal energy from a pot-bellied stove is transferred through the room by conduction, convection, and radiation. As the fuel burns, the chemical energy stored in the fuel is changed into thermal energy. The iron conducted the thermal energy, and the stove became hot. The heat from the stove is transferred to the air by convection currents. Warm air, which is less dense than cool air, is forced upward. This warm air rises until it reaches the ceiling, where it cools. Cool air is denser than warm air and, therefore, tends to sink. When the cool air nears the stove, it is warmed and the cycle repeats. Iron stoves also transferred thermal energy by radiation. Objects in the room absorb radiant energy from the stove, also causing the temperature of the room to rise.

Today, one of the most popular methods of home heating is central heating. **Central heating** is a system in which one heat source is used to heat an entire house or building. A hot air furnace is probably the most widely used form of central heating.

A hot air furnace is usually made of a metal firebox in which fuel such as coal, oil, or natural gas is burned. The firebox is sur-

A thermostat is a device that automatically responds to temperature change

rounded by a metal jacket filled with air. This jacket is connected to each room in the house or building by large tubes called air ducts. Heated air, because it is less dense than cool air, rises in the jacket and flows through the air ducts and into the rooms. Convection currents are established when the cold air in the room sinks and flows through the return ducts. In the furnace jacket, the cooler air pushes the hot air out into the ducts.

Another type of central heating system uses hot water instead of hot air. Convection currents similar to those in a hot air system carry hot water through pipes from the furnace to metal radiators in the room. How would thermal energy be transferred in a room with radiators?

Many hot air furnaces are equipped with an electric fan that forces hot air out of the furnace jacket and into the rooms. Electric fans can usually spread warmth faster and more efficiently than convection currents alone. The furnace is also equipped with a **thermostat,** a device that automatically responds to temperature changes in the rooms and activates switches that control the furnace.

The main part of most thermostats is made of metal, which expands when heated and contracts when cooled. When the metal is heated to a certain temperature, it expands and closes a valve that shuts off the supply of fuel. When the furnace has been off long enough to allow the thermostat to cool and contract, the valve opens and sends fuel to the burner. The burner is ignited by a small pilot light that remains lit at all times.

Another form of central heating is a heat pump. A **heat pump** is a heat mover that can work in two directions. A heat mover removes heat from an object at a high temperature and moves it to an object at a lower temperature. How does a heat pump work?

A heat pump contains a refrigerant, or cooling fuel, that moves through the pump. To heat an area, cool refrigerant in the pump removes thermal energy from outside air and delivers it to the inside of a home or building. To cool a home, a heat pump takes thermal energy from the air inside the house and moves it to the outside air, thereby cooling the house to a comfortable temperature. ■

Lesson Review

In the space provided, write the word or words that best complete the statement.

1. Before the pot-bellied stove, _____ were used to heat homes.

2. A stove that burns fuel such as coal or oil heats a room by _____,

   _____, and _____.

3. Warm air is _____ dense than cool air.

4. _____ is a system in which one heat source is used to heat an entire building.

5. The _____ of a hot air furnace is connected to each room in a building by air ducts.

6. A device that automatically responds to temperature changes and activates switches that control a furnace is a(n) _____.

7. A heat pump is a(n) _____ that can operate in two directions.

8. In order for a heat pump to heat an area, refrigerant in the pump _____ thermal energy from the outside of the building.

● 9. In the summer months, a heat pump can be used to _____ heat from a house.

● 10. Thermal energy is transferred by a hot air furnace primarily by _____.

Solar-Heating Systems

Today, much of the energy used to heat homes, run cars and other forms of transportation, light buildings and streets, operate factories, and cook food comes from fossil fuels. **Fossil fuels** are fuels such as coal, oil, and natural gas that formed millions of years ago from the remains of plants and animals. Fossil fuels take millions of years to form. Therefore, they are nonrenewable resources. **Nonrenewable resources** are materials from Earth that cannot be remade or replaced once they are used up. The burning of fossil fuels also is a major source of air pollution. What are the energy alternatives to fossil fuels?

Scientists estimate that the sun, the star that warms our planet, is about five billion years old and is only halfway through its life cycle. Therefore, the sun is one long-lasting alternative to fossil fuels. In fact, in less than one hour, the sun delivers more energy to Earth than all Earth's inhabitants use during an entire year! If the sun's energy can be used efficiently, the world's dependence on fossil fuels might be eliminated.

One method of tapping the sun's energy is using **solar collectors,** which are devices that collect the sun's radiant energy. Most solar collectors are black plates covered with glass or plastic. Black plates are used because dark-colored materials absorb radiant energy. The collectors are filled with water. An **active solar-heating system** is powered by pumps. Solar collectors absorb radiant energy from the sun and transfer this energy to the water in the collectors. The warmed water is then pumped to a storage tank. From the storage tank, the water is pumped to a heat exchanger that transfers energy to heat the building.

In a **passive solar-heating system,** energy is collected, distributed, and stored without using pumps. Greenhouses are passive solar-heating systems. The plastic or glass from which the greenhouse is made allows the radiant energy from the sun into the structure to warm the plants. The glass or plastic also keeps energy from escaping. Most buildings that use passive solar-heating systems have most of their windows facing south. Why?

The house above has solar collector panels on its roof. The workers on the left are installing photovoltaic cells on a building roof.

In what other ways can solar energy be used as an alternative to fossil fuels? Solar energy can be converted directly into electricity by devices called photovoltaic, or solar, cells. Most solar cells are made of materials that conduct heat. When sunlight strikes the cells, an electric current is produced.

Special mirrors called heliostats are also used to gather solar energy. Heliostats focus sunlight onto a receiving tower. Solar furnaces heated by heliostats can reach temperatures as high as 6,000° Fahrenheit! The heat that flows from the furnaces in the form of steam can be used to generate electricity.

Solar energy is a clean, long-lasting source of energy. Why is it not used more widely? One of the major problems with using solar energy is that, at night or during bad weather, there is little or no sunlight. Problems also exist with the storage of solar energy. Finally, at the present time, using solar energy is far more costly than using other fuels. ■

Heliostats focus sunlight onto a receiving tower at this solar power plant.

Lesson Review

Determine whether each of the following statements is true or false. Correct each false statement by crossing out the word or phrase that makes it false and by writing the correct word or phrase above it.

_____ 1. Currently, much of the energy used to heat homes comes from the sun.

_____ 2. Fossil fuels include coal, oil, and natural gas.

_____ 3. Nonrenewable resources can be remade or replaced in the very near future.

_____ 4. Our star, the sun, is a long-lasting source of energy to Earth.

_____ 5. Solar collectors are devices that collect the sun's kinetic energy.

_____ 6. In a passive solar-heating system, pumps are used to transfer energy.

_____ 7. A greenhouse is an active solar-heating system.

_____ 8. Solar cells cannot be used to convert the sun's energy into electricity.

● _____ 9. Solar cells made of plastic or glass would conduct more heat than those made of metals.

● _____ 10. A power plant that relies on solar energy would be more efficient in Maine than in Florida.

Welders use heat to fuse together both metallic and plastic surfaces.

Welders are people who use heat to fuse together, or weld, either metallic or plastic surfaces. It is estimated that about one million welders work in various industries in the United States. Most welders are employed in automobile plants, the aircraft industry, refineries, manufacturing plants, and on construction sites. Some welders work in independent metalworking repair shops. Government agencies, such as departments of public works, road commissions, and motor pools, also employ welders. Welding requires a steady hand, good eye-hand coordination, and great eyesight.

Ceramic engineers are scientists who work with nonmetallic, inorganic materials called ceramics. Ceramic materials must be able to withstand relatively high temperatures. Ceramics include those materials used to make electronic parts for calculators and computers, and heat-resistant parts for furnaces, cooking utensils, and dinnerware. Some ceramic engineers design parts that are used in nuclear reactors. Most ceramic engineers are employed by companies that manufacture glass or those that produce clay and stone products.

Sheet metal workers make and install ducts that are used in ventilating, air conditioning, and heating systems. Sheet metal workers are employed by factories that produce appliances such as freezers, refrigerators, stoves, and air conditioners. Some sheet metal workers own their own heating and air conditioning businesses. Others work with plumbers and electricians to assist in the installation and servicing of heating and cooling systems. Sheet metal workers are also employed by companies that install and maintain roofs.

Petroleum geologists work in the oil and natural gas industry. Many spend a considerable amount of their time looking for reserves of fossil fuels. Because fossil fuels are nonrenewable resources, the search for them is an ongoing task for petroleum geologists. In addition to locating new oil and gas fields, petroleum geologists monitor the production of existing deposits. By working with petroleum engineers, they are able to determine the amount of oil and gas still in the ground and can assist in developing better techniques to extract the oil and gas. Petroleum geologists can spend most of their time doing research in an office, or they can be found in the field on oil drilling rigs.

Many careers that depend upon heat and thermal energy are available to people with a general knowledge of science. People in all of the careers mentioned employ assistants and technicians. Some of the jobs that are available in this field are open to those who are willing to serve as apprentices at first. As the supply of fossil fuels dwindles, the need for qualified personnel in fields of energy alternatives is rapidly growing. ■

For Further Information

More information about these and related careers is available from the following publications and organizations.

Occupational Outlook Handbook,
U.S. Department of Labor

American Welding Society
550 NW LeJeune Road
Miami, FL 33126

American Association of Petroleum Geologists
P.O. Box 979
Tulsa, OK 74101

National Association of Trade and
Technical Schools
2021 K Street, NW
Washington, DC 20006

Magnetism and Electricity

Electromagnets are used in many electronic devices.

Magnetism

Ancient Greeks observed magnetism when they discovered that a black rock called lodestone attracted pieces of iron. You have probably observed magnetism when using an electric can opener, opening a kitchen cabinet, or hanging something on the refrigerator with a kitchen magnet. **Magnetism** is a property of some matter in which two objects are attracted, or pulled together, due to unlike poles.

Have you ever noticed that a bar magnet or a horseshoe magnet has a stronger attraction at the ends rather than in the middle? **Magnetic poles** are the places on a magnet where the magnetic forces are strongest. Every magnet has two poles. If a magnet is allowed to swing or to spin freely, one pole will point north and the other pole will point south. Magnetic poles are named for the

direction in which they point. The pole that freely points north is called the north pole. The south pole freely points south. Poles that point the same direction are called like poles. Like poles repel one another; unlike poles attract one another.

Compasses are made with magnets. The pointer of the magnet in a compass points north when the compass is in the Northern Hemisphere. The compass pointer points south in the Southern Hemisphere. Why? Earth is a magnet. Like all magnets, Earth has two magnetic poles. Earth's real magnetic pole is in northern Canada. The magnetic north pole is about 1,000 miles from Earth's geographic North Pole, the most northern place on Earth. Earth's magnetic south pole is in Antarctica, about 1,600 miles from the geographic South Pole.

30

All magnets, including Earth, have a magnetic field. A **magnetic field** is the area around a magnet where objects are attracted or repelled. Magnetic fields are invisible. However, if you cover a bar magnet with a sheet of paper and sprinkle iron filings onto the paper, the filings will fall into circular lines that show the force between the two poles of the magnet. These lines of force are the magnetic field.

What would happen if a magnet were broken into two pieces? Would each piece keep its magnetic property? What would happen to the magnet's poles? A **permanent magnet** is a magnet that keeps its magnetism. Most permanent magnets are made of steel, or of a mixture of iron and other metals. If a permanent magnet is broken into two pieces, each piece is still a magnet. The broken edges become new poles.

Magnets that lose their magnetism are called **temporary magnets.** When a pin is attracted to a bar magnet, the pin can attract other small pieces of metal. While attached to the bar magnet, the pin becomes a temporary magnet. However, when the pin is removed from the permanent magnet, the pin loses its magnetism.

An electromagnet is another temporary magnet. An **electromagnet** is a core of wire that has electricity flowing through it. If the electricity is stopped, the wire loses its magnetism. Electromagnets usually have a stronger magnetic field than permanent magnets. Thus, electromagnets have many uses. Electromagnets are used in small household appliances, electronic toys, televisions, cranes, industrial motors, computer equipment, stereo speakers, and other electrical devices. ■

Lesson Review

In the space before each number, write the letter of the word or group of words in Column 2 that matches the description in Column 1.

Column 1

_____ 1. the property of matter in which two objects are attracted due to unlike poles

_____ 2. the places on a magnet where the magnetic forces are the strongest

_____ 3. the pole of a magnet that points north

_____ 4. these poles repel one another

_____ 5. these poles attract one another

_____ 6. the area around a magnet where objects are attracted or repelled

_____ 7. a magnet that keeps its magnetism

_____ 8. a coil of wire through which electricity flows

● _____ 9. a paper clip attached to a magnet becomes one of these

● _____ 10. this part of a magnet will be pushed away from the south pole of another magnet

Column 2

a. electromagnet

b. like poles

c. magnetic field

d. magnetic poles

e. magnetism

f. north pole

g. permanent magnet

h. south pole

i. temporary magnet

j. unlike poles

Matter and Electricity

Have you ever experienced a slight "shock" from a doorknob after walking across a carpet on a cold, dry day? Have your socks ever "stuck" together as they were taken from the dryer? Have you ever heard a cracking sound as you pulled a wool sweater over your head in the winter? These examples are the effects of static electricity.

To understand any form of electricity, you must know something about matter. **Matter** is anything that takes up space and has mass. All matter is made of tiny particles called **atoms.** Some matter is made of only one kind of atoms. Gold is made of gold atoms. Iron is made of iron atoms. Some matter is made of more than one kind of atoms. Water is made of hydrogen atoms and oxygen atoms.

Every atom is made up of three kinds of even smaller particles called electrons, protons, and neutrons. An **electron** is a particle with a negative ($-$) charge. A **proton** is a particle with a positive ($+$) charge. A **neutron** is a neutral particle. Neutrons have no electric charge. All atoms have the same number of protons as electrons. The positive charges of the protons cancel out the negative charges of the electrons. Therefore, all atoms are neutral.

Most of the mass of an atom is in the **nucleus,** or the center core, of the atom. All of the atom's protons and neutrons are located in the nucleus. What kind of electrical charge does the nucleus have?

The electrons of an atom move around the nucleus of an atom in circular paths called orbits. Because they are outside the nucleus, electrons can be added or lost from an atom. Atoms that have either added or lost electrons are called **ions.** If an atom adds electrons, it becomes a negatively-charged ion. If an atom loses electrons, it becomes a positively-charged ion. Ions with unlike charges attract one another. Ions with like charges repel one another.

What happens to electrons, for example, if you rub a hard rubber comb with a piece of wool? Before you rub, both the comb and wool are neutral, or uncharged. As you rub the

Lightning is a form of static electricity that develops when large amounts of electrical charges build up in clouds.

objects together, electrons are moved from the wool to the comb. The extra electrons now on the atoms of the comb give it a negative charge. The loss of electrons on the atoms of the wool gives the wool a positive charge. The movement of electrons from the wool to the comb was a form of electricity. **Electricity** is energy caused by the transfer of electrons. The negative charge on the comb and the positive charge on the wool are examples of static electricity. **Static electricity** is the electrical charge built up in one place.

Lightning is caused by static electricity. Clouds often build up large electrical charges. Electrons flow from a negatively-charged area of the cloud to an area with a positive charge. This fast flow of electrons to a positively-charged area causes the electrical spark called **lightning.** Lightning can occur within one cloud, between two clouds, or between a cloud and Earth.

Lightning, like any electrical spark, produces heat and can cause fires. Lightning rods are devices that conduct electrical charges, or electrons, into the ground. Lightning rods are usually made of copper or other metals which are good conductors of electricity.

Static electricity has few practical uses. Once enough electrons have moved into a positively-charged area, the area becomes neutral and the flow of electrons stops. In order for electricity to be useful, the flow of electrons must continue. A continuous flow of electrons is called **current electricity.** Current electricity lights houses and other buildings, starts cars, and runs a vast number of appliances, including stoves, hair dryers, televisions, radios, and telephones. ■

Lesson Review

In the space provided, write the word or words that best complete the statement.

1. _____ is energy caused by the transfer of electrons.

2. Anything that takes up space and has mass is called _____.

3. A particle of an atom which has a positive electric charge is a(n) _____.

4. The number of _____ and the number of electrons in a neutral atom is the same.

5. If an atom loses electrons, it becomes _____ charged.

6. Rubbing a hard rubber comb with a piece of wool causes the movement of _____ from the _____ to the _____.

7. Lightning is a form of _____ electricity.

8. _____ electricity is a continuous flow of electrons.

● 9. The nucleus of an ator has a _____ charge.

● 10. Table salt is made of two ions, sodium and chlorine, which are attracted to each other. The sodium ion has a positive charge. The chlorine ion has a _____ charge.

Current Electricity

Current electricity was first used commercially in 1858 when a lighthouse lamp was illuminated in Dover, England. Recall that current electricity results from the continuous flow of electrons. Current electricity is one of the most important forms of energy available. It provides light for reading, runs appliances, powers industrial machines, and runs commuter trains. How do you depend upon electricity?

The flow of electrons or other charged particles through a conductor is an **electric current.** There are two types of electric currents: direct and alternating. In a **direct current,** or DC, the electrons flow in only one direction. Direct current is used in all batteries, including those that power flashlights, portable radios, and automobiles. In an **alternating current,** or AC, electrons flow first in one direction and then in the opposite direction. Alternating current powers most cities, factories, and homes. The current in most homes is about 60-cycle AC. In a 60-cycle current, electrons change direction 60 times per second.

A current will flow only if there is an unbroken path for electrons to follow and a source of electric energy is present to move the electrons along the path. The path followed by electrons from the source to the output device, such as a lamp, is called a **circuit.** A complete circuit includes a source of electrical energy; a path for conducting the electrons, usually copper wire; and a device to use the electricity. A short circuit is caused when an electrical current cannot flow through all parts of a circuit. Worn electrical cords, broken light switches, overloaded outlets, and improperly working appliances are common causes of short circuits. Short circuits can cause electrical sparks that lead to a fire.

The battery, a commonly used source of

electrical energy, is made of one or more cells. A **dry cell** usually is made from chemical paste, a small carbon rod, and a zinc container. The rod is the positive part of the cell. The negative part of the cell is the zinc container. The chemical paste contains ions that allow the flow of electrons from the zinc container to the carbon rod. Dry cell batteries are used in flashlights, portable radios, and some calculators.

A **wet cell** consists of two metal plates in an acidic solution. In a wet cell, a chemical reaction between the acid and the metal plates allows the acid to conduct electrons. Most automobiles are powered by a wet-cell battery.

Electrons flow from one end, or terminal, of a battery, to the device that uses electricity, and back to the other battery terminal. The potential difference between the electrons at the negative terminal and the electrons at the positive terminal of a battery is the **voltage.** Voltage is measured in units called volts. The

Worn electrical cords must be replaced to avoid dangerous short circuits.

voltage in most homes is either 110 or 220 volts. An ordinary two-cell flashlight operates on three volts.

The rate at which an electric current flows is the **amperage.** The ampere, or amp, is the unit used to measure how much electricity flows through a circuit over a period of time.

Recall that power is the work done by a machine divided by the time required to do the work. Electrical power is called wattage.

The unit of power is called a watt. **Wattage** is the voltage multiplied by the amperage.

When you pay your electrical bill, you are paying for kilowatt-hours, abbreviated kwh, of electricity used. One kilowatt equals 1,000 watts. A **kilowatt-hour** is a measure of the thousands of watts used in one hour. In the United States, an average household uses between 650 to 850 kwh of electricity per month. ■

Lesson Review

Fill in the circle containing the letter of the term or phrase that correctly completes each statement.

1. In a(n) _____ current, electrons flow in only one direction.
   - ⓐ alternating
   - ⓑ short
   - ⓒ direct
   - ⓓ kilowatt

2. Homes and other buildings use _____ current.
   - ⓐ alternating
   - ⓑ short
   - ⓒ direct
   - ⓓ kilowatt

3. The path followed by electrons from the electrical source to the output device is a _____.
   - ⓐ battery
   - ⓑ dry cell
   - ⓒ wet cell
   - ⓓ circuit

4. A _____ is caused when an electrical current cannot flow through all parts of a circuit.
   - ⓐ dry cell
   - ⓑ short circuit
   - ⓒ wet cell
   - ⓓ all of the above

5. A(n) _____ is made from chemical paste and a carbon rod inside a zinc container.
   - ⓐ amperage
   - ⓑ wet cell
   - ⓒ dry cell
   - ⓓ volt

6. The potential difference between electrons at the negative terminal and electrons at the positive terminal of a battery is the _____.
   - ⓐ voltage
   - ⓑ kilowatt-hour
   - ⓒ amperage
   - ⓓ watt

7. Wattage is the _____.
   - ⓐ voltage multiplied by amperage
   - ⓑ voltage divided by amperage
   - ⓒ amperage multiplied by 1,000 watts
   - ⓓ amperage divided by 1,000 watts

8. One kilowatt equals _____ watts.
   - ⓐ 10
   - ⓑ 100
   - ⓒ 1,000
   - ⓓ 10,000

● 9. A current of five amps flows through a toaster connected to a 110-volt source. The power used by the toaster is _____ watts.
   - ⓐ 105
   - ⓑ 115
   - ⓒ 550
   - ⓓ 1,000

● 10. A broken prong on the end of an appliance cord can cause a _____ if it is plugged into a source of electricity such as an electrical outlet.
   - ⓐ magnet
   - ⓑ fire
   - ⓒ direct current
   - ⓓ wet cell

Using Electricity

A glowing light bulb and the heat from an electric iron are only two of the many uses of electricity. Electrical devices convert electrical energy into other forms of energy. Appliances such as fans and mixers convert electricity into mechanical energy. Lamps change electricity into light and thermal energy. How does electricity provide light and heat?

Electricity does not flow freely through a circuit. There is always some opposition to the flow of electrons, just as there is opposition to the movement of a wheel over the surface of a road. The opposition to the flow of an electrical current is **resistance.** The resistance of an electrical current is an opposing force similar to friction. Resistance produces thermal energy, which is converted into heat.

Resistance depends upon the length and thickness of the conductor and the type of material from which the conductor is made. Copper wire offers little resistance and therefore is a good conductor of electrical current. Glass and rubber, on the other hand, offer high resistance and are poor conductors of electricity.

Resistance is measured in ohms. The mathematical relationship among resistance, voltage, and current is called Ohm's law. According to Ohm's law, the current in amperes is equal to the voltage divided by the resistance. An increase in current causes an increase in voltage at a given resistance.

To most people, the production of light is an important use of electricity. Light bulbs change electrical energy into radiant energy, or light, and thermal energy. If you look closely at a clear light bulb, you will notice a coil of very thin wire in the center of the bulb. When the bulb is part of an electrical circuit, this coil becomes white hot and produces light.

Electricity can also be converted into mechanical energy. **Electric motors** are machines that change electrical energy into mechanical energy. Electric motors range in size from the tiny motors that drive model trains to the large motors used by real locomotives. Electric motors convert electrical energy to mechanical energy in household appliances, such as blenders, mixers, fans, electric can openers, and vacuum cleaners, to name just a few.

You have learned that electrical energy can be changed into thermal energy, radiant energy, and mechanical energy. How is electrical energy transferred from power plants to your house? The most common source of electricity for houses is a generator. **Generators** are machines that convert mechanical energy into electrical energy. Power plants use enormous generators to produce electrical

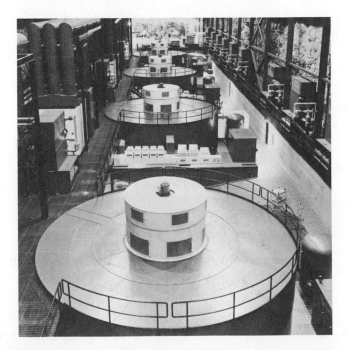

These turbine units are part of a pumped-storage hydro plant that generates electricity.

energy. The electrical energy is then sent through power lines that can carry extremely high voltage over great distances. To counteract the resistance of the lines, the voltage must be increased at certain points along the way. However, to be usable, the voltage must be decreased before delivery to a building. **Transformers,** devices that increase or decrease voltage, are located at various places along the electric-transport system.

Once electricity is delivered to a house at a usable voltage, it enters a circuit. There are two types of circuits: a series circuit and a parallel circuit. A **series circuit** provides a single path along which electricity flows to the objects that use it. In a series circuit, if one output device fails, all the other output devices also fail. For example, if five light bulbs are connected in series and one burns out, none of the four remaining bulbs will work. The voltage in a series circuit is equal to the sum of the electrical sources that feed into it. Two nine-volt batteries, for example, will make an 18-volt series circuit.

A **parallel circuit** provides two or more paths for a current to follow before it returns to its source. If five lamps in a room are connected to a single parallel circuit, one or more may burn out without interfering with the others. The current flows to each lamp individually. Parallel circuits are used in most houses because a parallel circuit permits all devices to use the same voltage. ■

Lesson Review

In the space provided, write the word or words that best complete the statement.

1. Electrical devices change _____ energy into other forms of energy.

2. The opposition to the flow of an electrical current is _____.

3. Resistance depends on the _____ and _____ of the conductor and the type of material from which the conductor is made.

4. Ohm's law states that current is equal to the voltage divided by the _____.

5. Light bulbs convert electrical energy into _____ and _____ energy.

6. _____ are machines that change electrical energy into mechanical energy.

7. _____ are machines that convert mechanical energy into electrical energy.

8. A _____ circuit provides two or more paths for a current to follow.

● 9. A thick copper wire will provide _____ resistance than a thin copper wire.

● 10. Three nine-volt batteries in a series circuit will provide _____ volts of energy.

Electronics

Electronics is the branch of science that uses magnetic and electrical principles to design electronic devices. Common electronic devices include radios, televisions, calculators, stereo systems, and computers.

Electronic devices do not use an electrical current to create an immediate and practical result, such as the light that lights your room, the sound that comes from your radio, or the answers that appear on your calculator. Electronic devices change the way current usually behaves by changing it into signals. The signals relay numbers, pictures, sounds, or other kinds of information. In radio and stereo systems, for example, the signals represent sounds. In television sets, the signals stand for both sounds and pictures. What do the signals in computers and calculators represent?

Have you ever heard someone refer to a radio as a "transistor radio"? A **transistor** is a part of an electronic device that changes

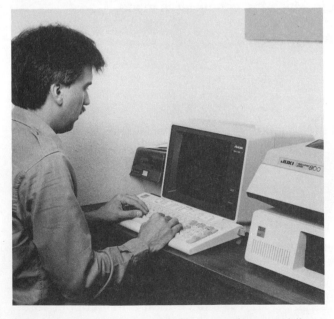

Computers with microprocessors work as rapidly and as accurately as larger computers. They can easily fit on the top of a desk.

electrical current into signals. Transistors are found in most of the radios, televisions, and stereo systems in use today. Transistors perform three main electronic functions: rectification, amplification, and oscillation.

Rectification is the simplest electronic operation. Rectification makes it possible for current to flow only in one direction. Recall that alternating current, or AC, is a current in which the electrons flow in one direction and then in another. Most buildings have alternating current. All electronic equipment, however, needs direct current, or DC, to operate. A transistor called a **rectifier** changes AC into DC.

Amplification is an electronic function that amplifies, or strengthens, a signal. An **amplifier** is a transistor that builds a weak signal into a strong signal. Amplifiers are used in televisions, stereo systems, navigational equipment, and medical equipment.

A transistor called an **oscillator** converts direct current into signals that operate on a particular frequency. Oscillators are used by radio and television stations to produce the high frequencies needed to send their sounds and pictures over great distances. Oscillators also produce signals to control many computers. These types of transistors are also used to create the high-frequency waves used in radar systems and microwave ovens.

Many kinds of electronic equipment still use individual transistors to perform basic electronic functions. The most modern equipment, however, uses integrated circuits. An **integrated circuit** is a circuit that includes all of the rectifiers, amplifiers, oscillators, and other kinds of transistors needed to operate an electronic device. All of these transistors are connected and pressed onto a tiny, silicon chip called a **microchip.** A chip that is only two-tenths of an inch square can hold an integrated circuit large enough to power a watch. Other microchips are no larger than the head of a pin. Such a tiny integrated circuit may easily contain over 1,000 transistors.

Modern electronic equipment that operates with integrated circuits is far smaller than older equipment. It also costs less to buy and operate than devices that use individual transistors. Integrated circuits add to the lifetime of electronic equipment that uses them. Large electronic equipment, such as a stereo system or a microcomputer, may need many integrated circuits to perform a variety of tasks. Thus, most microchips include tiny, metal contacts that allow them to be connected to other chips.

What kinds of electronic devices do you use every day that make your life easier or more convenient? A computer may be among the items you use. What is a computer? A **computer** is an electronic device that solves complex problems by breaking them down into simpler problems. The first computers were so large and expensive that their benefits were limited to large organizations.

In the early 1970s, electronics researchers developed the microprocessor. A **microprocessor** is a single integrated circuit that can perform all of the mathematical calculations of much larger computers. A microprocessor also stores large amounts of information in the computer's memory. Computers with microprocessors work as accurately and as rapidly as large computers, yet they cost much less and fit easily onto the top of a desk. ∎

Lesson Review

In the space before each number, write the letter of the word or group of words in Column 2 that matches the description in Column 1.

Column 1

_____ 1. these change current into signals that relay pictures, sounds, or information

_____ 2. a part of an electronic device that changes the electrical current into signals

_____ 3. a transistor that changes AC into DC

_____ 4. a type of transistor that strengthens a signal

_____ 5. this includes all the transistors of an electronic device

_____ 6. a tiny piece of silicon that holds an integrated circuit

_____ 7. an electronic device that solves complex problems by breaking them down into many simpler problems

_____ 8. a single integrated circuit that can perform all of the calculations of a larger computer

• _____ 9. a device used to turn signals back into sounds

• _____ 10. these are represented by the signals in calculators

Column 2

a. amplifier

b. computer

c. electronic devices

d. integrated circuit

e. microchip

f. microprocessor

g. numbers

h. radio

i. rectifier

j. transistor

Electrical technicians who work for power companies often monitor the operation of generating equipment and transformers.

Electrical engineers work with the production and use of electricity. Many electrical engineers work for power companies, where they design power-generating equipment and supervise its operation. Other electrical engineers supervise the operation of the equipment that delivers electricity to customers. These engineers redesign electrical systems in those areas where the demand for electricity is increasing. They also develop maintenance programs and direct electrical repairs and rebuilding operations. Electrical engineers can also work for manufacturers of electrical equipment and for construction companies. Others work for companies that provide general engineering services.

Electrical technicians work in jobs that deal with the generation, transmission, and use of electrical power. They usually work for one or more electrical engineers. Some electrical technicians work for power or telephone companies. Those who work for power companies often monitor the operation of generating equipment and transformers. Electrical technicians also work for manufacturers of electrical equipment, where they assemble electrical parts, test them, and make design changes with the assistance of an electrical engineer.

Electronics engineers work with equipment that uses very small amounts of electricity. Such equipment includes computers, telephone systems, radar, television, and home entertainment products. Electronics engineers come up with ideas for new equipment and plan the development of the equipment. They monitor equipment performance and develop mainteance and repair programs. Most electronics engineers work for companies that manufacture electronic equipment. Some work for federal agencies, such as the Department of Defense and the Federal Aviation Administration.

Electronics technicians test, install, and repair a wide variety of electronic equipment. They often work with electronics engineers on the design of electronic equipment. Electronics technicians work for private companies that manufacture such equipment. Some technicians work in the assembly and testing of the equipment. Others are customer service technicians who install and repair electronic equipment in customers' homes and offices.

The electrical energy field offers many career opportunities. Electrical contractors employ licensed electricians and electricians' assistants who install and service circuits in houses and commercial buildings. Power companies hire people to work in line maintenance and repair. Electronics firms employ engineers, technicians, and support people. People with a good knowledge of electricity can also find jobs in all levels of government. ■

For Further Information

More information about these and related careers is available from the following publications and organizations.

Careers in the Electrical, Electronics, and Computer Engineering Field, Institute of Electrical and Electronics Engineers, 1983

Opportunities in Microelectronics Careers, D. Mike Horning and Richard Moran, National Textbook Company, 1985

National Society of Professional Engineers
1420 King Street
Alexandria, VA 22314

Electronic Industries Association
2001 Eye Street, NW
Washington, DC 20006

American Society for Engineering Education
11 Dupont Circle, NW
Washington, DC 20036

Light

Visible light is only a small part of the electromagnetic spectrum.

The Electromagnetic Spectrum

What do light, sound, and X rays have in common? All transfer energy by means of waves. A **wave** is a rhythmic disturbance that carries energy. A wave is made of several parts. The high point of a wave is called the crest. The low point is the trough. The distance from one trough to the next or from one crest to the next is the **wavelength.** The number of waves that pass a given point in one second is called the **frequency.** Waves with high frequencies have short wavelengths. Waves with low frequencies have long wavelengths.

Some forms of energy, such as electricity, are transferred through matter. **Electromagnetic waves** do not have to travel through matter to transfer energy. Light waves and radio waves can transfer energy without using matter. The arrangement of electromagnetic waves according to their frequencies is the **electromagnetic spectrum.**

Light is the part of the electromagnetic spectrum with which you are most familiar.

Surprisingly, not all light can be seen. Light that people can see is called visible light. The rainbow shows the colors of visible light, or the visible spectrum of light. The visible spectrum includes red, orange, yellow, green, blue, indigo, and violet light. The longest wavelength visible to the human eye is red light, which is about 0.000030 inches, or 30 millionths of an inch. The shortest wavelength visible is violet light, which is 0.000015 inches, or 15 millionths of an inch.

Light with wavelengths longer or shorter than visible light is invisible light. Invisible light with wavelengths too long to be seen includes radio waves and infrared light. Invisible light with wavelengths too short to be seen includes ultraviolet light, X rays, and gamma rays.

The waves with the longest wavelengths are **radio waves.** Radio waves carry music and other forms of sound to your radio. Radio waves also make it possible to watch your favorite television programs. Radio waves with a short wavelength are called microwaves. Microwaves cook food very quickly.

Electromagnetic waves with a wavelength just a little longer than those of visible light are **infrared waves.** Infrared radiation is given off by all hot objects and is used to keep foods warm and soothe sore muscles.

Ultraviolet light, or UV light, has a shorter wavelength than visible light. UV light is emitted by extremely hot objects, such as our sun and other stars. Ultraviolet light from the sun helps your body to produce vitamin D. Ultraviolet light also kills bacteria. Therefore, it is used in hospitals to sterilize surgical tools

and operating rooms. Food manufacturers use UV light to sterilize food containers.

X rays are radiant energy with a wavelength shorter than UV light. X rays can pass through certain materials, such as wood, skin, leather, and some metals. X-ray photographs detect broken bones, tooth decay, and abnormal tissue growths in the body. X rays are also used to treat many diseases.

The electromagnetic waves with the smallest wavelength and the highest frequency are **gamma rays.** Gamma rays are produced in the nuclei of certain atoms. Gamma rays have a very short wavelength and are able to penetrate almost any material. ■

Lesson Review

On the line before each statement, write the letter of the choice that best completes it.

_____ 1. A(n) _____ is a rhythmic disturbance that carries energy.
   a. frequency   b. wave   c. magnet   d. wavelength

_____ 2. The distance from one wave trough to the next wave trough is the _____.
   a. frequency   b. crest   c. wavelength   d. rhythm

_____ 3. The longest wavelength visible to the human eye is _____ light.
   a. blue   b. orange   c. green   d. none of the above

_____ 4. Light with wavelengths too short to be seen by the eye include _____.
   a. UV light   b. X rays   c. gamma rays   d. all of the above

_____ 5. The electromagnetic waves with the longest wavelengths are _____.
   a. radio waves   b. X rays   c. gamma rays   d. microwaves

_____ 6. _____ are used to keep food warm and soothe sore muscles.
   a. X rays   b. Infrared waves   c. Radio waves   d. Gamma rays

_____ 7. _____ can kill bacteria.
   a. UV light   b. Radio waves   c. X rays   d. Gamma rays

_____ 8. _____ are produced in the cores of atoms.
   a. X rays   b. Frequencies   c. Wavelengths   d. Gamma rays

● _____ 9. The color that corresponds to the shortest wavelength visible is _____.
   a. red   b. green   c. violet   d. all of the above

● _____ 10. _____ are used at airport security stations to detect hidden weapons in bags.
   a. Radio waves   b. X rays   c. Infrared waves   d. Gamma rays

Light—Visible Radiation

Recall that light is the only visible part of the electromagnetic spectrum. Light is produced when atoms absorb energy from an outside source and release this energy as light. Visible light can be natural or artificial, depending upon how it is produced.

Most of the visible light that you see comes from the sun. The sun and other stars are luminous objects. Luminous means "light-giving." **Luminous objects** are those that produce and emit, or give off, their own light. Although the moon appears to glow in the night sky, it is not a luminous object. In fact, the moon, Earth, and the eight other planets in our solar system only appear to glow because they reflect light from the sun.

Why do fireflies glow? Why does a lighted wick of a candle glow? Why does a light bulb shine? **Luminescence** is the emission of visible light as the result of life, or biological processes, a chemical reaction, friction, or electrical energy. Fireflies, some jellyfish, and certain mushrooms glow in the dark. These objects are bioluminescent. They give off light because of their biology. When kerosene lamps burn petroleum products or when a candle is lit, luminous flames are produced through chemical reactions. When electricity flows through the wire filament of a light bulb, the filament becomes white hot and produces light.

Luminescence, or light, that continues only while an outside source emits radiation is **fluorescence.** A fluorescent lamp produces light only as long as the ultraviolet light bombards the special coating on the inside of the light tube. Neon signs are also fluorescent. High voltage electric current flowing through neon-filled tubes causes the neon gas to glow and produce light.

Luminescence that continues after the radiation of light stops is **phosphorescence.** Phosphorescent light may last for a fraction of a second, or for days, depending on the material giving off the light. Some watch and clock dials are coated with a phosphorescent material. Egg shells, certain minerals, and some types of glue are also phosphorescent.

Why can't you see around corners? What causes your shadow? Light travels in a straight line. You can't see around corners because light cannot turn corners. Shadows are cast because light cannot pass through or around most solid objects.

Materials through which light will not travel are called **opáque.** Wood, stone, and metals are opaque materials. Materials that allow some light to pass through are called **translucent** materials. Translucent materials diffuse, or break up, light. Tissue paper and frosted glass are translucent. Materials

Table 1	
Mean Distances of the Planets from the Sun	
Mercury	36,000,000 miles
Venus	66,800,000 miles
Earth	93,000,000 miles
Mars	142,500,000 miles
Jupiter	480,000,000 miles
Saturn	885,000,000 miles
Uranus	1,700,000,000 miles
Neptune	2,754,000,000 miles
Pluto	3,666,000,000 miles

In a vacuum such as space, light travels at the speed of 186,000 miles per second. How long does it take sunlight to reach each of the planets in our solar system?

that allow light to travel completely through them are **transparent.** Unpolluted air, clean water, and ordinary window glass are transparent materials.

The speed of light depends upon the type of material through which it travels. In space, which is a vacuum, light travels at 186,000 miles per second. Light slows down when it hits Earth's atmosphere or any other type of matter. Earth is about 93 million miles from the sun. Thus the light from the sun reaches Earth in about eight minutes! Due to the vastness of space, scientists use the speed of light to measure large distances. These distances are measured in **light-years,** the distance that light travels in one year. A light-year equals nearly 6,000,000,000,000, or six trillion, miles! ■

Lesson Review

Fill in the circle containing the letter of the term or phrase that correctly completes each statement.

1. Most of the visible light you use comes from _____.
   - (a) the sun
   - (b) the moon
   - (c) bioluminescent objects
   - (d) candles

2. The emission of visible light as the result of certain biological processes, chemical reactions, or electricity is _____.
   - (a) artificial light
   - (b) transparent
   - (c) opaque
   - (d) luminescence

3. Neon signs are _____.
   - (a) a biological process
   - (b) phosphorescent
   - (c) bioluminescent
   - (d) fluorescent

4. Shadows are cast because light _____.
   - (a) is visible radiation
   - (b) is reflected from your body
   - (c) cannot travel through solid objects
   - (d) none of the above

5. _____ is the speed of light in space.
   - (a) 186,000 miles/second
   - (b) 186,000 miles/day
   - (c) 186,000 miles/hour
   - (d) 186,000 miles/year

6. Most distances in space are measured in _____.
   - (a) feet
   - (b) yards
   - (c) miles
   - (d) light-years

7. _____ materials do not transmit any light.
   - (a) Opaque
   - (b) Translucent
   - (c) Transparent
   - (d) Glassy

8. Frosted glass is a(n) _____ material.
   - (a) opaque
   - (b) translucent
   - (c) transparent
   - (d) radiant

9. Light from a flashlight is _____.
   - (a) luminescent
   - (b) a biological process
   - (c) transparent
   - (d) opaque

10. "Glow-in-the dark" T-shirts give off light because they are _____.
    - (a) phosphorescent
    - (b) opaque
    - (c) transparent
    - (d) translucent

Reflection

You can see an object only when light travels from that object to your eyes. For you to see this page, light must first strike the page and be reflected to your eyes. **Reflection** occurs when light strikes an object and bounces away from it.

Nearly everything you see is reflected light. For example, when you stand in front of a flat mirror, you can see your own reflection and the reflections of objects around you. These images, or reflections, are upright but reversed from left to right. The reflections also appear as the same sizes as the objects that make them. They also appear to be as far away from the mirror as the actual objects. You can see yourself and the other images because almost all the light that strikes the mirror is reflected back to your eyes. How are these images produced?

Look at the illustration. When light rays strike a flat mirror at an angle, they are reflected away at the same angle. The angle at which light rays strike a smooth surface is called the **angle of incidence.** The angle at which the rays bounce away from the mirror is called the **angle of reflection.** The angle of incidence always equals the angle of reflection.

A sharp, clear image is formed only when light rays are reflected from a very smooth surface such as glass, still water, or polished metal. What happens when light strikes a rough surface? When light strikes a rough surface, the rays are reflected away in many directions.

Not all mirrors are flat mirrors. A **convex mirror** is a mirror that is curved like the back of a spoon. Look at the back of a metal spoon. This surface is a convex mirror. Like a flat mirror, a convex mirror forms an upright image that appears to be behind the

mirror. But unlike the image formed by a flat mirror, the image in a convex mirror is smaller than the object actually is.

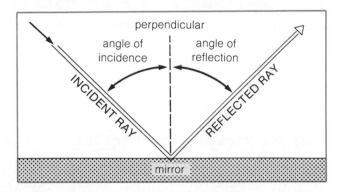

When light is reflected from a smooth surface, the angle at which it strikes the surface equals the angle at which it is reflected from the surface.

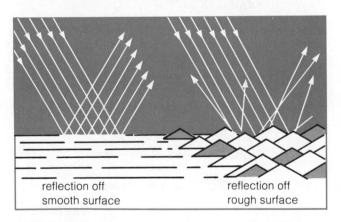

Light is scattered when it strikes a rough surface.

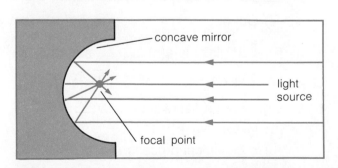

Light striking a concave mirror is reflected to a focal point.

Convex mirrors are sometimes used as rearview mirrors in automobiles because they provide a wider field of view than flat mirrors produce. A caution statement is usually printed on these mirrors. Why? Images of the objects reflected in convex mirrors are smaller than the actual objects. Therefore, the objects appear to be much farther away than they actually are.

A **concave mirror** is a mirror that is curved like the bowl of a spoon. Light reflected from a concave mirror comes together at one place called the focal point, which is located in front of the mirror. The orientation and size of the image formed by a concave mirror depends upon the distance the object is from the mirror. The image might be upright, or it may be upside down. It may be actual size, or larger or smaller than the object. The image also appears to be either behind or in front of the mirror producing it. Describe your image as it appears in the bowl of a metal spoon.

Common uses of concave mirrors are as reflectors in flashlights and car headlights. Reflecting telescopes use concave mirrors to collect light from the sky and project images of stars, planets, and other space objects. Probably the most famous reflecting telescope is the one housed in the Mount Palomar Observatory. Its main mirror is 200 inches in diameter. ■

Lesson Review

Determine whether each of the following statements is true or false. Correct each false statement by crossing out the word or phrase that makes it false and by writing the correct word or phrase above it.

_____ 1. To see an object, light must first strike the object and then be reflected from it to your eyes.

_____ 2. An image in a flat mirror is always upside down.

_____ 3. The angle at which light strikes a smooth surface is the angle of reflection.

_____ 4. A sharp, clear image forms only when light strikes a rough surface.

_____ 5. A convex mirror is a mirror that is curved like the back of a spoon.

_____ 6. The image formed by a convex mirror is always larger than the object that produces the image.

_____ 7. A concave mirror is a mirror that is curved like the bowl of a spoon.

_____ 8. Concave mirrors are used as flashlight reflectors.

● _____ 9. Due to the behavior of light, you are able to see yourself in a smooth blanket of snow.

● _____ 10. Your image in the back of a metal spoon is always smaller than you are and is upright.

Refraction

Recall that light waves travel at different speeds through different materials. Light travels through space at the speed of 186,000 miles/second. Light slows down slightly when it passes through transparent matter such as air, water, or glass. When light rays pass from one transparent material to another, the rays are bent and change speed. **Refraction** is the bending of light rays that occurs when light passes through certain materials.

Have you ever noticed that a straw in a glass of water appears bent? Light travels more quickly through air than through water. The slowing down of light rays makes the straw appear to bend where the air and water meet. In what other everyday situations can you observe the refraction of light waves as they travel from the air into another material?

Light is refracted in instruments such as eyeglasses, microscopes, certain telescopes, and cameras through the use of lenses. A **lens** is any curved, transparent material that refracts light rays. Most lenses are made of either glass or plastic. There are two kinds of lenses: convex lenses and concave lenses.

A **convex lens** is a lens that is thicker in the middle than it is at its edges. Recall that light travels in a straight line. When light enters a convex lens, the rays are refracted, or bent, toward the focal point, a place where the bent rays come together. Magnifying glasses, camera lenses, and your eyes are convex lenses.

What if you held a magnifying glass near the wall directly opposite a window on a sunny day? If the lens is moved slowly away from the wall, the image of the window will be projected on the wall. The image, however, appears inverted, or upside down.

A camera works the same way. Light rays passing through the shutter of the camera are refracted, or bent, by the lens and focused onto the film. The image formed on the film is smaller than the object producing it and is inverted. A slide projector works on the same principle. To view slides in their proper orientation, how should you insert them?

Each of your eyes has a flexible, convex lens that focuses an image on the retina, a light-sensitive tissue that acts like the film in a camera. You can see an object only after its image has been converted into nerve impulses on your retina and transmitted to your brain.

You can see an object clearly only if the image is focused exactly onto the retina. Many

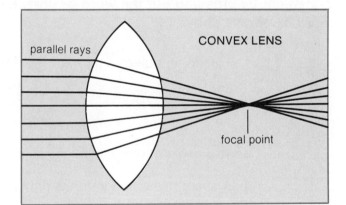

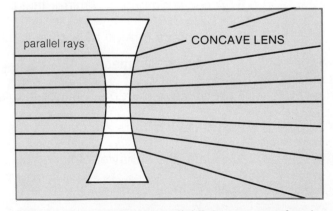

Convex lenses refract parallel light rays to a focal point. Concave lenses spread parallel rays apart.

people have eyes that are misshapen. When the eyes are not shaped correctly, the lenses focus images either in front of or behind the retina, producing blurred images.

When the images of distant objects form behind the retina, the eyes are farsighted. Farsighted people can focus clearly on objects far away from them. Farsightedness can be corrected with eyeglasses with convex lenses.

When the images of distant objects form in front of the retina, the eyes are nearsighted. Eyeglasses with concave lenses are used to correct this eye disorder. A **concave lens** is a lens that is thinner in the middle than it is at the edges. When light enters a concave lens, the light rays spread apart. Concave lenses cannot focus light. ■

Lesson Review

On the line before each statement, write the letter of the choice that best completes the statement.

_____ 1. Light travels through _____ at 186,000 miles per second.

    a. glass   b. water   c. air   d. space

_____ 2. _____ is the bending of light rays as they pass through certain materials.

    a. Reflection   b. Magnification   c. Refraction   d. Imaging

_____ 3. Light is refracted in instruments such as _____.

    a. camera lenses   b. microscopes   c. eyeglasses   d. all of the above

_____ 4. _____ lenses are thicker in the middle than at the edges.

    a. Convex   b. Mirror   c. Concave   d. Nearsighted eyeglass

_____ 5. When light rays enter a convex lens, they are bent _____.

    a. toward the focal point   c. toward the source of the light rays

    b. away from the focal point   d. none of the above

_____ 6. The image produced by a convex lens is _____.

    a. upright   b. blurred   c. inverted   d. all of the above

_____ 7. The light rays that enter a camera lens are focused on the _____.

    a. retina   b. film   c. concave lens   d. image

_____ 8. A(n) _____ lens cannot focus light.

    a. convex   b. concave   c. camera   d. telescope

● _____ 9. When standing waist deep in water, your legs look shorter because of _____.

    a. water depth   c. refraction of light as it enters the water

    b. reflection of light bouncing off water   d. nearsightedness

● _____ 10. To have your vacation slides projected onto the screen in upright orientations, you must put the slides into the projector _____.

    a. upright   c. backwards

    b. upside down   d. all of the above

Color

You probably recognize most objects by their shape and color. Two objects with identical shapes are easily distinguished from one another if they are different colors. For example, two of your neighbor's cars may be the same make, model, and age. But you can tell at a glance the red car from the blue car. What is color, and how is it produced?

Color is just one of the many properties of light. **White light,** or ordinary sunlight, is a mixture of many colors. White light can be separated into the visible spectrum with a prism. A **prism** is a transparent object that refracts, or bends, light rays into the visible spectrum. Recall that the visible spectrum includes red, orange, yellow, green, blue, indigo, and violet light, and the many shades of these colors.

Suppose you take a prism and hold it into a beam of sunlight. What happens? The prism refracts the sunlight and separates it into the seven main colors of the visible spectrum. The colors may also blend to form red-orange, blue-green, and others. A rainbow is formed in the same way. When tiny drops of water in Earth's atmosphere hang in the air after a rain, they act as prisms to refract sunlight into the colors of the visible spectrum.

Each color of the spectrum refracts, or bends, at a different angle. Look at the illustration. Notice that violet light is refracted at a greater angle than red light. Is blue light refracted at a greater or lesser angle than green?

What if you held a convex lens in the path of the rays emerging from the prism? Recall that a convex lens is a lens that is thicker in the middle than it is at the edges. The convex lens converts the refracted, colored light back into parallel beams of white light.

Then, why is the sky blue? Why is an orange orange? Why is a lemon yellow? The color of an object depends upon the light that is reflected away from, or bounced off, that object. The sky is blue because it reflects more blue light than it does other colors of light. Most of the other colors of light are absorbed by the atmosphere that makes our sky. In white light, an orange appears orange because it absorbs most light and reflects orange light back to your eyes. What color of light is reflected by a lemon?

What about black and white objects? A white cloud appears white because it reflects all the colors of the visible spectrum. A piece of coal appears black because it absorbs all the colors of the spectrum.

What color would the cloud be if you were to view it through sunglasses with blue lenses? The white cloud would appear blue because white objects reflect the color of the light through which they are viewed. What color would a red apple appear to be if you were to shine a blue light on it? The red apple will reflect only red light. However, since there is only blue light to be reflected,

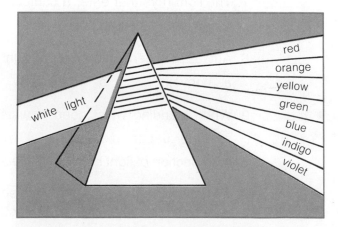

Sunlight, or white light, can be separated into its component colors with a prism.

the apple would absorb all the colors of light shining on it and so the apple would appear to be black in color.

It is important to remember the effects of light on color when shopping. A shirt or dress will appear to be one color under the artificial lighting. In sunlight, however, the clothing will appear to be slightly different colors. Artificial light also affects the colors of makeup and of photographs taken indoors.

What color are your car's taillights? What color is your grass after a week of spring showers? Red and green are the obvious answers to these questions. However, to some people these colors appear only as shades of dull brown or gray that look very similar. The condition is called colorblindness. People who are colorblind cannot see all the colors of the visible spectrum or are unable to distinguish among certain colors. Red-green colorblindness is an inability to tell the difference between red and green. In another form of colorblindness, green is seen as gray and red is seen as yellow. Colorblindness is an inherited condition that is more common in men. Nearly ten percent of American males have some form of colorblindness. Less than half of a percent of American women are colorblind. ■

Lesson Review

In the space provided, write the word or words that best complete the statement.

1. _____, or sunlight, is a mixture of many colors.

2. A transparent object that refracts light rays into the visible spectrum is a(n) _____.

3. The main colors of the visible spectrum, in the order in which they appear, include

_____, _____, yellow, green, _____,

indigo, and _____.

4. A rainbow forms when tiny _____ in Earth's atmosphere act

as prisms to refract sunlight.

5. The color of an object depends upon the light that is _____ from

the object.

6. A white object appears white because it reflects _____ colors of the

visible spectrum.

7. A black object appears black because it _____ colors of the visible

spectrum.

8. _____ is an inherited condition in which a person is unable to see

certain colors or is unable to distinguish among certain colors of the visible spectrum.

● 9. Because colors are used in traffic lights, most states test to determine if a person has

_____ colorblindness before issuing a driver's license.

● 10. When photographed in green light, a clown's white face would appear to be

_____ in color, and her orange wig would appear _____.

Other Properties of Light

You have learned that light is a wave, or a rhythmic disturbance, which carries energy. Recall also that light can be reflected from, refracted by, or absorbed by an object. What are some other properties of this type of electromagnetic radiation?

Recall that the high part of a wave is called the crest and the low part of a wave is the trough. If two or more light waves combine so that the crest of one wave matches the crest of another wave, the two waves are in phase with one another. However, if the crest of one wave fits into the trough of another wave, the waves are out of phase. The ability of two or more waves to combine to form a new wave is **interference.**

You have more than likely observed interference of water waves that occurs when a rock is thrown into a pond or into a pool of standing water. The waves appear to form concentric circles around the point where the rock entered the surface of water. Light waves are affected by interference in a similar manner. The display of color on a soap bubble or on a spot of oil are examples of the results of interference of light waves.

Another property of light is diffraction. **Diffraction** is the bending of light waves that occurs when they pass through an opening or around the edges of an object. You can observe diffraction by passing a beam of light through a narrow slit in a piece of cardboard or a thin piece of wood. You will notice that most of the light passes through the slit. Light near the edges of the slit, however, spreads out in circles.

Diffraction has a "blurring" effect. Observe the shadow made by putting your hand under the bulb of an ordinary lamp. You will notice that the shadow of your hand has soft, blurred edges.

A **diffraction grating** is a surface of numerous, very small, evenly spaced, parallel slits. Some diffraction gratings can have as many as 15,000 slits per inch. When light of one color passes through a diffraction grating, it is diffracted, or bent and blurred. An interference pattern of dark and light bands forms. The size of the space between the bands depends upon the color of light that is passed through the grating. Violet light makes the smallest spaces. What color of light produces the largest spacings? White light produces all the colors that are seen in the visible spectrum.

Do you own a pair of polarized sunglasses? How do they reduce the glare of sunlight? The lenses that are used in polarized sunglasses are made of special filters. The molecules that make up the filters are lined up in such a way that they resemble parallel slots. If two pieces of polarized filter are placed back to back and lined up so that their slots are parallel, sunlight can readily pass through the slots. If one piece of the polarized filters is turned at an angle of 90° to the other, however, light is absorbed and the glare from the sunlight is greatly reduced.

So far, you have learned about the wave properties of light. Light also behaves like particles. When radiation collides with matter, the radiation behaves as a particle. Visible light and all other forms of electromagnetic radiation are made of particles called photons. **Photons** have no mass, yet they have energy and travel through space at a speed of 186,000 miles per second. ∎

Fill in the circle containing the letter of the term or phrase that correctly completes each statement.

1. The high part of a wave is called the _____ and the low part of a wave is called the _____.

   ⓐ trough, crest   ⓑ crest, photon   ⓒ crest, trough   ⓓ photon, crest

2. Light waves are in phase with one another when the crest of one wave coincides with _____.

   ⓐ the trough of that same wave   ⓒ the crest of the same wave

   ⓑ the trough of another wave   ⓓ the crest of another wave

3. The ability of two or more waves to combine together to form a new wave is called _____.

   ⓐ interference   ⓑ diffraction   ⓒ photon   ⓓ polarizing

4. The display of colors on a soap bubble or on a spot of oil is an example of the _____ of light waves.

   ⓐ polarizing   ⓒ diffraction

   ⓑ interference   ⓓ all of the above

5. _____ is the bending of light waves that occurs when light passes through an opening or around the edges of an object.

   ⓐ Diffraction   ⓑ Interference   ⓒ Photoning   ⓓ Absorption

6. A(n) _____ is a surface of many, very small, evenly spaced, parallel slits through which light can pass.

   ⓐ polarized light   ⓒ wave crest

   ⓑ interference   ⓓ diffraction grating

7. The lenses that are used in polarized sunglasses are made of special light _____.

   ⓐ waves   ⓑ filters   ⓒ photons   ⓓ particles

8. Light is made of tiny particles called _____ that travel through space at 186,000 miles per second.

   ⓐ electrons   ⓑ protons   ⓒ photons   ⓓ neutrons

● 9. The play of colors on the surface of a record album that occurs when white light is reflected is an example of _____.

   ⓐ photoning   ⓑ polarization   ⓒ diffraction   ⓓ interference

● 10. When _____ light is passed through a diffraction grating, all of the visible colors of the spectrum are seen.

   ⓐ black   ⓑ red   ⓒ violet   ⓓ white

Lasers

You may have heard about the use of lasers in surgery to cut out diseased and damaged tissue. Lasers are used to repair damaged retinas in the human eyes. Laser beams also are used in supermarkets to scan bar codes on products. You may have seen a laser light show. What are lasers? How are they produced?

A **laser** is a device that produces an intense, narrow beam of light that is all one wavelength and therefore one color. The word *laser* is an acronym for **l**ight **a**mplification by **s**timulated **e**mission of **r**adiation. What does this mean? Recall that light is a form of electromagnetic radiation. Laser light is light that is strengthened, or amplified.

Atoms become excited when they absorb energy. Excited atoms can return to their normal energy levels by giving off light. Light that is emitted, or given off, irregularly is referred to as spontaneously emitted light. Spontaneously emitted light, such as light from the sun or light from a flashlight, is called incoherent light. **Incoherent light** is light in which the waves travel in different directions and have different wavelengths.

Excited atoms can give off light systematically in a process called **stimulated emission.** Stimulated emission occurs when the energy released by one atom combines with the energy of another atom to produce coherent light. **Coherent light** is light in which all the light waves travel in the same direction and have the same wavelength. Laser light is coherent light.

All lasers have a power source, usually electricity, which supplies energy to a solid, a liquid, or a gas. The solid, liquid, or gas through which the energy passes is called the active medium. The active medium used to produce the laser beam determines the intensity and the color of the beam. For example, a ruby crystal will produce a red laser beam. A gas such as carbon dioxide produces an invisible beam.

The nature of laser light allows it to be used in communications and other industries, medicine, and research. Because of the high frequency of a laser, or the high number of waves that pass a given point in one second, a laser beam used in the communications industry can carry more information than radio waves. In fact, a laser beam can transmit as many as ten million telephone calls at once. Laser beams also can be used to carry signals of many television programs.

A special lens can be used to focus a laser beam to a point as small as one

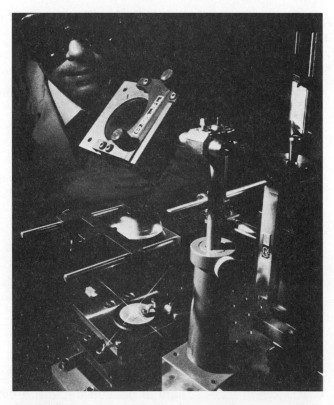

A high-power laser bores a precise hole in a pellet of silicone.

ten thousandth of an inch in diameter. This extreme concentration of light can produce temperatures of over 10,000°F. Thus, in industries such as steel making, lasers can be used to cut and weld metals.

In medicine, lasers are used to vaporize parts of a single cell, thus permitting micro-surgery of certain cell parts. Lasers are also used to destroy cancerous tissue without damaging neighboring, healthy tissue. Less blood is lost in surgeries that use laser beams because the light seals small blood vessels as it cuts through skin and tissues. Laser surgery is completely germ-free and greatly reduces the chances of infection because none of the equipment ever touches the patient.

Laser beams have many other applications. Some ships and planes, for example, use lasers to determine the speed and direction of approaching vessels to avoid collisions. In fact, many commercial planes and ships are beginning to use laser range finders and guidance systems. Scientists have used lasers to measure distances in space. What are some other uses of laser beams? ∎

Lesson Review

Determine whether each of the following statements is true or false. Correct each false statement by crossing out the word or phrase that makes it false and by writing the correct word or phrase above it.

_____ 1. Lasers produce a beam of light that is many wavelengths and colors.

_____ 2. Laser light is radiation that is strengthened, or amplified, by the object producing the light.

_____ 3. Spontaneously emitted light is coherent light.

_____ 4. Coherent light is light in which all the light waves travel in the same direction and have the same wavelength.

_____ 5. The source of most lasers is usually electricity.

_____ 6. A ruby crystal produces an invisible laser beam.

_____ 7. A laser beam has a low frequency.

_____ 8. Laser surgery is sterile because the equipment never touches the person, decreasing the risk of infection.

● _____ 9. Laser surgery helps increase the blood lost during surgery.

● _____ 10. Laser light focused through a special lens can produce temperatures much hotter than sunlight.

Photography requires a good understanding of light and optics.

Physicians are medical professionals who are concerned with human health. Physicians care for and treat people with illnesses and diseases. They also help people stay in good health. Many physicians work in private practice. Others work in clinics with other physicans who have similar specialties. Physicians use many kinds of electromagnetic waves to treat their patients. Because X rays can pass through certain materials, they are often used to study the condition of human tissues, bones, and organs. Infrared rays may be used to treat some skin diseases and to soothe sore muscles. Some physicians use laser light to perform surgery.

Photographers use visible light, infrared waves, mirrors, and lenses to create scenic landscapes, portraits, and other kinds of photographs. Photography requires a good understanding of light and optics. Many photographers are self-employed, doing work for a variety of businesses, including advertising agencies, and publishing and printing companies. Many photographers own and operate studios that provide photographs for weddings, graduations, and other special events. Some photographers work for museums and assist in the development of displays. Other photographers use their skills to produce photographic art.

Ophthalmologists are physicians who specialize in the care and treatment of the human eye. These physicians are able to prescribe drugs to treat diseases of the eye.

Some ophthalmologists perform surgery to correct vision, remove diseased or damaged tissue, or repair detached retinas. Ophthalmologists often employ optometrists who examine people's eyes and prescribe lenses and exercises to correct vision problems. Most optometrists supply, fit, and adjust eyeglasses and contact lenses. In certain states, optometrists are licensed to use drugs to treat the eyes.

Thin-section technicians grind and polish rocks and minerals to thicknesses that can be viewed with certain kinds of microscopes. A thin-section technician uses polarized light to determine the transparent minerals present in a rock. Polished surfaces are made of the opaque components and are viewed with reflecting microscopes. Thin-section technicians are employed in geology departments at colleges and universities. Others work in the petroleum and mining industries.

Many career opportunities exist in the vast number of jobs that use radiant energy. For example, radiologic technicians who take and develop X rays are an integral part of most medical staffs. Other technicians use X rays to treat certain diseases. Photographers either develop their own film or hire assistants to do so. Ophthalmologists and optometrists often work with dispensing opticians who are responsible for supplying and fitting eyeglass frames. Thin-section technicians may work with other kinds of laboratory assistants to produce a finished product. ∎

For Further Information

More information about these and related careers is available from the following publications and organizations.

Peterson's Guide to Engineering, Science, and Computer Jobs, Peterson's Guides, 1988

Occupational Outlook Handbook, U.S. Department of Labor, 1988

American Medical Association
535 N. Dearborn Street
Chicago, IL 60610

American Geological Institute
4220 King Street
Alexandria, VA 22302

Professional Photographers of America, Inc.
1090 Executive Way
Des Plaines, IL 60018

Sound

Modern communication equipment allows almost instant communication with the entire world.

Sound

Look around you. What do you see? Recall that light enables you to see the many different objects around you. Now, sit perfectly still. Close your eyes. What do you hear? Depending upon where you are, you might hear the hum of traffic from a nearby highway, the chirping of birds, the ticking of a clock, or the sound of voices or footsteps from a nearby hallway. What is sound? How is sound like light?

Light is a wave, a rhythmic disturbance that carries energy. Light is a transverse wave. A **transverse wave** is a wave in which matter moves at right angles to the direction the wave travels. Transverse waves can be made by holding both ends of a spring and shaking one end up and down. The wave travels along the spring. Note that the spring only moves up and down.

Like light, sound is a wave. However, it is a compressional wave. A **compressional wave** is a wave in which matter vibrates in the same direction as the wave travels. Compressional waves can be made by pinching together several coils of the spring and releasing them. Note that the wave travels back and forth along the spring, but the spring does not move up and down.

The frequency of a wave is the number of waves that pass a given point in one second. Frequency is measured in a unit called hertz, which is abbreviated Hz. One hertz is equal to one wave per second. Most people can produce vocal sounds between 85 and 1,100 hertz. People can hear sounds within the range of 20 to 20,000 Hz. A dolphin can produce sounds within the range of 7,000 to 120,000 hertz.

58

The **intensity** of a sound is the amount of energy that is in the sound wave. **Loudness** is a person's response to the intensity of a sound. Loudness is measured in units called decibels. Normal whispers are about 15 decibels loud. A noisy restaurant reaches 85 decibels. A plane leaving the runway to become airborne produces sounds of over 150 decibels.

Unlike light, sound waves travel only through matter. The speed of sound depends upon two factors: the kind of matter through which the sound travels, and the temperature of the matter. At about 70°F, sound travels through air at about 1,100 feet per second. However, at 32°F, sound travels through air at a little less than 1,000 feet per second.

Sound travels through water that is about 70°F at about 5,000 feet per second. Sound travels through steel at a speed of over 17,000 feet per second.

At 186,000 miles per second, light travels much faster than sound. How can you prove this? Have you ever noticed that during a thunderstorm, lightning is always seen before thunder is heard? In fact, due to the different speeds of light waves and sound waves, you can estimate how far away the storm is by counting the seconds between the flash and the thunder. In air, sound travels about one mile in five seconds. If you count 15 seconds between the flash and the thunder, how far away from you is the lightning? ■

Lesson Review

In the space before each number, write the letter of the word or group of words in Column 2 that matches the description in Column 1.

Column 1

_____ 1. a wave in which matter travels at right angles to the direction of movement

_____ 2. a wave in which matter travels in the same direction as movement

_____ 3. the number of waves that pass a given point in one second

_____ 4. one wave per second

_____ 5. a whisper is about this loud

_____ 6. the amount of energy in a sound wave

_____ 7. a person's response to the intensity of a sound

_____ 8. this type of energy wave travels only through matter

• _____ 9. sounds with this frequency can be heard by humans

• _____ 10. sound travels through this type of matter more quickly than through liquid

Column 2

a. compressional

b. frequency

c. hertz

d. intensity

e. loudness

f. 15 decibels

g. 7,000 hertz

h. solid

i. sound

j. transverse

Other Characteristics of Sound

Recall that all sound waves are compressional waves produced by vibrating matter. But what causes the multitude of different sounds that you are able to distinguish? Why is the high, piercing sound of an ambulance siren quite different from the low, rumbling sound of a fog horn on a coastal lighthouse? Why does the same note played on the trumpet, violin, and piano sound different? The difference in sounds made by different objects is due to the type of matter the object is made from and the way in which the object vibrates.

When a trumpet is blown, the musician's vibrating lips cause a column of air inside the metal instrument to vibrate and thus produce sound. Friction between a moving bow and a string of a violin creates sound by setting the string in vibrating motion. The vibrating string, however, produces only very faint sounds. When the string vibrates against the wood, the wood amplifies, or strengthens, the sound's loudness. Sound from a piano is produced when downward pressure on a key causes a small hammer to strike and vibrate a particular string.

Each of the sounds described above is produced by vibrations. However, the material used and the method used to produce the sound cause the distinct sounds each instrument makes. The characteristic of sound that allows you to identify the sound with a certain source is the sound's **quality.** Sound quality is related to loudness and pitch. Recall that the intensity of a sound is related to the amount of energy being transferred. Loudness, in turn, describes a person's response to intensity.

Pitch, or shrillness, is the way in which a person hears the frequency of a sound. Recall that frequency is the number of waves that pass a given point in one second. High-pitched sounds have faster frequencies than low-pitched sounds. Sounds with very high pitches, such as chalk scraping against a chalkboard, are shrill. The sounds made by a bass guitar, on the other hand, are sounds with low, deep pitches.

What appears to be a change in the pitch of a sound either due to the movement of the source of the sound or the movement of the listener is called the **Doppler effect.** While waiting at a railroad crossing, you may have noticed that the pitch of the locomotive horn seems higher as the train nears the crossing. Then, as the train moves farther

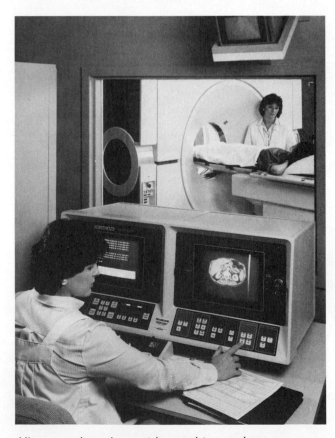

Ultrasound equipment is used to produce an image of unborn babies.

from the crossing, the pitch seems to lower. Why does this happen?

Recall that sound waves travel through air at about 1,100 feet per second. Sound from the train horn is traveling at this speed. As the train approaches the crossing, however, the sound waves from the horn become crowded together. Because the waves now have a shorter distance to travel to your ears, the pitch appears higher. Then, as the train leaves the crossing, the waves become farther apart and take longer to reach your ears. Therefore, the pitch of the horn seems lower. How is the horn pitch heard by passengers on the train?

Recall that people can hear sounds within the range of 20 to 20,000 hertz. Sounds with frequencies higher than 20,000 hertz are called **ultrasounds.** You are probably most familiar with the use of ultrasounds on pregnant women. Ultrasounds can be reflected from the fetus to produce an image of the fetus on a screen. Doctors then are able to check the development of the fetus without risk to it or the mother. Ultrasounds can also be used to clean delicate medical instruments. At certain frequencies, ultrasounds can produce enough energy to weld certain metals.

Ultrasounds are also useful to animals other than humans. Certain bats, for example, can hear sounds within the range of 1,000 and 120,000 hertz. These bats produce ultrasounds in the form of cries that bounce off nearby objects and return to the bats as echoes. The echoes help the bats to avoid running into objects and assist them in finding food. ■

Lesson Review

Identify each of the following statements as true or false. Correct each false statement by crossing out the word or phrase that makes it false and by writing the correct word or phrase above it.

_____ 1. The same note on different musical instruments sounds different because of the method used to produce the sound and because of the material from which the instrument is made.

_____ 2. Sound quality is related to loudness only.

_____ 3. Loudness is the way in which a person hears the frequency of a sound.

_____ 4. Very high-pitched sounds are shrill.

_____ 5. High-pitched sounds have faster frequencies than low-pitched sounds.

_____ 6. An apparent change in pitch due to the motion of an object making the sound or the motion of the listener is called the Ultrasound effect.

_____ 7. Because of their frequencies, ultrasounds can damage a fetus.

_____ 8. Certain bats use ultrasounds to find food.

● _____ 9. Singing a musical scale from low to high is an example of changing pitch.

● _____ 10. People on a train hear no change in pitch of the train's horn as the train approaches and leaves a crossing.

Noise and Music

Your taste in music is probably much different from that of another generation such as your parents' or grandparents'. In fact, tastes in music vary greatly among members of the same generation. What you consider music may be considered noise by someone else. What you believe sounds pleasant, others may consider unpleasant. What makes music different from noise—other than personal taste?

Differences among sounds are due to differences in quality, loudness, and pitch. It may be surprising to learn that not all sounds have these three characteristics of quality, loudness, and pitch. For example, the sound of colliding automobiles certainly has a loudness that can be measured. The frequency of the vibrations of this sound, however, is too irregular to produce definite quality and pitch. Sound with irregular vibrations, or wave patterns, is called **noise.**

Any source can produce noise. Most human speech has a definite quality, loudness, and pitch. Loud shouts or hissing sounds, however, produce irregular wave patterns and are therefore noise. Certain animal sounds such as the chirping of birds produce a definite pitch. Cows mooing, on the other hand, is classified as noise. The sound of a violin when played properly can be very melodic and very pleasing to the ear. A beginning violinist, however, is sure to produce noise before becoming skilled at playing the instrument. Again, music is a matter of personal taste. Some people find the bagpipes pleasing; others find this kind of music shrill and unpleasant. Asian music is soothing to some people and irritating to others.

How are the sounds called music produced? There are hundreds of different musical instruments. All of them, however, can be classified into three major groups based on how the instrument produces sound. The three groups of musical instruments are: percussion, wind, and stringed instruments.

Percussion instruments produce sound as a result of being struck. Drums, xylophones, cymbals, and bells are percussion instruments. When these instruments are hit, they vibrate. The vibrations cause changes in pressure of the air near the instruments. The air begins to vibrate. Your ears hear these vibrations as sound. Most percussion instruments do not produce a definite pitch and thus are often called rhythm instruments. Rhythm instruments are used to strengthen the beat of a musical work.

Wind instruments produce sounds from columns of air that vibrate within the instruments. The air needed to produce the sounds for most wind instruments comes from the person playing the instrument. In a trombone, the musician's lips cause the vibrations. In a clarinet, a wooden reed helps to produce sound. A flute produces sound when the person playing it blows into the mouthpiece.

The pitch of a wind instrument depends upon the length of the column of air. Air vibrating in a short instrument will produce a higher pitch than air vibrating in a longer instrument. A trumpet is shorter than a French horn. Which instrument will have a higher pitch?

Stringed instruments produce sounds because a string has been plucked or moved with a bow. The plucked string vibrates, causing the air that surrounds it to vibrate. A guitar produces sound when the strings are plucked with the fingers or with a pick. Most stringed instruments that are plucked have between six and 12 strings. A violin, on the other hand, produces sound when a bow is drawn over the strings. Most stringed instruments played with a bow have four strings. A cello has four strings. Is it plucked or played with a bow?

The pitch of a stringed instrument may be changed in a way similar to the way pitch is changed in a wind instrument. In a wind instrument, the length of a column of air affects a sound's pitch. On a stringed instrument, pitch is changed by changing the length of the vibrating string. The shorter the string is, the higher the pitch will be. Pitch is changed on a stringed instrument by pushing down on the strings with the fingers. Pitch can also be controlled by changing the diameter of the strings or by increasing or decreasing the tension of the strings.

The human voice is a combination of a wind instrument and a stringed instrument. The **larynx,** or voice box, is located in the upper area of the trachea. The **trachea** is a tube that carries air to the lungs. The larynx is made of cartilage and contains the vocal cords. Air passing between the vocal cords causes them to vibrate. The vibrating cords and the movements of the tongue and the mouth produce sounds. ■

Lesson Review

In the space provided, write the word or words that best complete the statement.

1. Differences in sound are due to differences in _____, _____, and pitch.

2. Sound with irregular vibrations, or wave patterns, is _____.

3. The chirping of birds has a definite pitch and therefore can be classified as _____.

4. The sounds made by cows are classified as _____.

5. _____ instruments produce sound as a result of being struck.

6. Instruments that produce sound with vibrating columns of air are _____ instruments.

7. Guitars and violins are _____ instruments.

8. The movements of the human tongue and mouth and vibrating _____ produce sounds.

● 9. A trumpet has a _____ pitch than a trombone.

● 10. A tuba is a _____ instrument.

Acoustics

You have probably gone to a play, a lecture, or some other gathering where you weren't able to understand the person speaking. Although you might have seen the speaker's lips moving and perhaps heard the person's voice, the sound you heard may not have been distinct. In fact, the sounds you heard may have been a rumbling and meaningless noise. Recall that noise is sound that has irregular wave patterns or vibrations. Someone sitting a few rows away, however, may have had no problem understanding the speaker. Why?

Acoustics is the science that studies sound. Acoustic scientists study how sounds are produced and how sounds affect people. They also study the way in which certain materials absorb and reflect sound waves. Often, the word *acoustics* is used to describe the way in which sounds are absorbed or reflected by a certain material or the materials that make up a building or a room. What happens to sound in a particular area has puzzled scientists and architects for hundreds of years. Some areas of acoustics have still not been fully explained. However, many problems in the area of acoustics have been solved in recent years.

Sound waves can change paths when they strike an object. Sound is reflected from, or bounced off, smooth, hard surfaces. Rooms with ceilings or walls of brick, tile, or metal reflect most sound waves. Sounds made in rooms constructed from these materials bounce back and forth off the walls of the rooms. A listener hears the sounds many times before they are finally absorbed. The result of the many reflections of the sound waves is called **reverberation.** Reverberated sound is made up of many **echoes,** or reflected sounds, which are traveling so close together that no single echo can be heard. What is heard is a continuous rumble of sound.

Sound waves can also be absorbed. Soft, rough surfaces absorb most sound waves. The walls and ceiling of a soundproof room, such as a broadcasting room or a recording studio, are made of materials that absorb sound. Carpet and other soft materials also absorb sound.

Most theaters and auditoriums are designed to provide quality acoustics. The walls, ceilings, and chairs are often covered with soft materials that absorb some of the sounds produced. These materials also reduce reverberation. In addition to the materials in the room, the walls and ceilings of many theaters and auditoriums are curved in such a way that sound waves are reflected at different angles to produce better acoustics.

Why might a person a few rows away from you at a gathering have no problems understanding the speaker? You may have been seated in a **dead spot,** an area where hearing is very difficult or even impossible. While you are seated in a dead spot, the sound of one word might reach your ear at the same moment as the sound of another word because of the reflection of sound waves off the walls or ceilings of the room. The sounds tend to cancel each other, resulting in either no sound at all or a rumbling noise. A person sitting outside the dead spot would probably not hear this interference. Recall that interference is the ability of two or more waves to combine to produce a new wave.

The acoustics of most buildings today are carefully planned before construction begins. Acoustic quality is also tested during many phases of the building process. If the building or room is to be used for speeches, plays, or concerts, its size and shape are carefully considered. The ability of its ceiling, floors, and walls to keep out unwanted sound is measured. Furnishings made out of sound-absorbing materials are chosen. Acoustic engineers do everything possible to control echoes so that dead spots are minimal.

In an auditorium designed for speaking, steps are taken to be sure that reverberations do not last for more than a second. In a hall designed for music, the room is planned and furnished to be sure that reverberations do not last for more than two seconds. Good acoustics do not come about by accident. They are planned. What type of design should be used for factories and other workplaces in which loud sounds may be damaging to those who work there? ■

Lesson Review

On the line before each statement, write the letter of the choice that best completes the statement.

_____ 1. _____ is sound that has irregular wave patterns.

    a. Acoustics   b. Reverberation   c. Noise   d. Echo

_____ 2. The science that studies sound is _____.

    a. Absorption   b. Echoing   c. Reflection   d. Acoustics

_____ 3. Rooms with walls and ceilings made of _____ reflect sound waves.

    a. metal   b. tile   c. brick   d. all of the above

_____ 4. Reverberated sound is made of many _____.

    a. frequencies   b. acoustics   c. echoes   d. none of the above

_____ 5. Sound waves are absorbed by _____.

    a. carpet   b. drapes   c. pillows   d. all of the above

_____ 6. A(n) _____ is an area where hearing is difficult or even impossible.

    a. echo   b. dead spot   c. soundproof room   d. recording studio

_____ 7. _____ is the ability of two or more waves to combine to produce a new wave.

    a. Echoing   b. Absorption   c. Acoustics   d. Interference

_____ 8. Concert halls usually have _____ chairs.

    a. padded   b. wooden   c. steel   d. brass

● _____ 9. Factories whose manufacturing processes produce loud noise should have rooms made of materials that _____ sound waves.

    a. reflect   b. absorb   c. echo   d. reverberate

● _____ 10. If you yelled toward the face of a tall cliff, you would be able to produce a(n) _____.

    a. silence   b. acoustic   c. echo   d. dead spot

Communicating with Sound

About 150 years ago, the ability to use speech to share information was limited by distance. If a person was too far away to hear your voice, you could not speak to that person. Written communication was the only method available to exchange information with distant people, and it often took weeks or months for such a message to be delivered.

In the nineteenth century, Samuel F. B. Morse experimented with electricity and electromagnets. In 1832, he developed a **telegraph,** a device that uses a complete electrical circuit to send messages over distances. A complete electrical circuit includes a source of electrical energy, a means of conducting electrons, and a device that uses the electricity. A telegraph system uses a sending key and a receiving set to transmit messages. The sending key breaks the circuit when pushed down, and the receiving set, or magnetic sounder, clicks out the message. Clicks made close together are called dots. Clicks farther apart are called dashes. Specific combinations of dots and dashes, called Morse code, are used to represent the letters in the alphabet.

Eventually, the telegraph key and sounder were replaced by the teletype machine, an electronically controlled typewriter. A message typed on the keyboard of one teletype machine can be sent to another teletype machine and typed onto paper by the receiving machine. Today, these machines have been largely replaced by computers.

What other devices allow you to communicate with sound? The telephone is one of the most commonly used communication devices. A telephone consists of a transmitter and a receiver connected by an electrical circuit. Telephones transmit the human voice and other sounds over great distances.

When you speak into a modern telephone, you are speaking into the transmitter. The sound waves from your voice strike a thin, round metal disk called a diaphragm. The diaphragm vibrates at the same frequencies as the sounds of your voice. Behind the diaphragm is a small cup containing pieces of carbon through which an electric current flows. As the diaphragm vibrates, the resistance of the carbon to the flow of electricity is increased and decreased. The current carries the sound waves produced by your voice and transmits them over the telephone wires. The part of the telephone through which you hear is called the receiver. The receiver converts the electrical impulses from the wire into sound waves. Both the telegraph and the telephone rely on wires for long distance communication.

The first radio was called a "wireless telegraph" because it transmitted sound through the air. Have you ever been to a radio station? If so, you have probably seen the disk jockey speak into a microphone. A **microphone** changes sound waves into electrical impulses at the sending station. Special equipment amplifies and varies the waves and sends them through the air in all directions from the station's antenna. An antenna in a receiving radio picks up the waves. A device called an oscillator changes the radio waves back into electrical impulses. The impulses go through a loudspeaker that transmits the sound.

In the early 1980s, telephone and radio communication combined to produce the cellular mobile telephone. A **cellular mobile telephone** makes it possible to make and receive calls from a moving car. A cellular telephone system is divided into smaller areas called cells. Each cell has a radio transmitter and receiver that operates on low

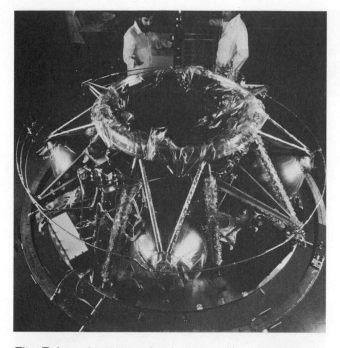

The Telstar 3 communications satellite relays signals around the world.

power. As a car with a cellular phone travels from one cell to another, a computer transfers the sound from one cell to another without interrupting the message.

More recently, a branch of physics called fiber optics has made it possible to use light to send voice messages faster than they can be sent with electricity or with radio waves. Fiber optics changes the electric telephone signals into light impulses or lasers. These signals are then changed back into sound waves at the receiving end.

Since 1960, **communications satellites,** spacecraft that orbit Earth and carry communication equipment, have been important in sound and visual communications. These satellites relay radio, telephone, and television signals among ground stations. Signals can be sent back and forth within one country or can be relayed from one country to another. ■

Lesson Review

In the space provided, write the word or words that best complete each statement.

1. A(n) _____ uses a sending key and a receiving set to transmit messages.

2. In Morse code, clicks that are close together are called _____.

3. A(n) _____ machine is an electronically controlled typewriter.

4. A telephone consists of a transmitter and a _____ connected by a wire.

5. A(n) _____ changes sound waves into electrical impulses at a radio sending station.

6. A(n) _____ in a receiving radio picks up radio waves.

7. A cellular mobile telephone uses a _____ to transfer radio waves from one cell to another without interrupting the message.

8. _____ has made it possible to send voice messages using light.

● 9. In order for a person in the United States to talk to a person in Germany over the telephone, a(n) _____ satellite must be used.

● 10. Using fiber optics is more efficient than using communications satellites because light travels _____ than sound.

Noise Pollution

If you happen to live far from a city, noise and other unwanted sounds probably don't bother you very often. Static, or "white noise," might interfere with a radio or television broadcast from time to time. A car without its muffler might drive past your house, creating unwanted sound. A plane passing overhead might produce an occasional loud rumble. If you live in or near a city, however, you are probably very much aware of noise that city life brings to the surroundings. **Noise pollution** is unwanted, disturbing, or harmful sounds.

One of the most common sources of noise pollution is motor vehicles. The noise produced by a single car or truck may not be particularly disturbing. However, when hundreds or thousands of automobiles, buses, trucks, and motorcycles are in a relatively small area, they create a disturbing level of noise. The intensity of noise from the constant stop and go of heavy traffic can easily exceed 100 decibels.

Noise pollution by motor vehicles isn't necessarily due only to large numbers of vehicles in a given place. For example, the car that lost its muffler produces unwanted sound as it cruises up and down the street. Most trucks contribute to noise pollution as they use their low gears to climb hills. Motorcycles also produce unwanted sounds affecting their operators and passers-by.

People who live close to busy airports are exposed to noise pollution often up to 15 or more hours per day. Communities near runways are bothered by the very loud noise of jet engines as planes take off and land. A plane leaving a runway approaches a noise level of 150 decibels. By comparison, the activities in an average house produce only 50 decibels of sound.

Construction projects can create a lot of noise.

Many industrial plants also contribute to noise pollution. Some factories use machines that are so loud that they can be heard far from the plant. How does this noise affect workers within the plant? The high levels of noise in such factories can pose serious physical and mental problems for workers. Exposure to loud noises for long periods of time can cause not only permanent hearing loss, but also can produce mental stress. Loud noises often make it difficult for people to concentrate on what they are doing. Constant noise makes accidents more likely to occur.

Music is a matter of personal taste. Technically speaking, however, many rock concerts are sources of noise pollution. The amplified sound from an average rock band approaches a loudness of 120 to 130 decibels. This level of sound intensity can produce permanent hearing loss.

Fortunately, some noise pollution is only temporary. Traffic jams often exist only during rush hours. Airline traffic is somewhat limited to certain hours a day and certain places. People who work in noisy factories are exposed to the noise only during work hours. Other sources of noise pollution, such as construction projects and emergency sirens, usually last for only short periods of time.

How can you protect yourself from noise pollution? One way is to prevent the noise from reaching you. Ear protectors can be used if you are constantly exposed to loud sounds and noise. Another way to limit the noise that reaches you is to decrease its loudness. Mufflers help to deaden the noise made by vehicles and machines. Fences that absorb and reflect sound have been designed and erected along stretches of busy highways.

Some people must work in noisy factories. Others have no choice but to live near busy airports. Traffic jams are a fact of life in many cities. How much noise is too much?

The federal government has established certain regulations and recommendations that address the problem of noise pollution. Workers in noisy factories should be exposed to noise of 90 decibels for only eight hours per day. Machines that produce louder noises have shorter exposure times. In many places, through truck traffic is prohibited in residential areas where alternate routes are available. Many large airports require planes to follow noise-limiting procedures. In what other ways might noise pollution be reduced? ∎

Lesson Review

Determine whether each of the following statements is true or false. Correct the false statements by crossing out the word or phrase that makes it false and by writing the correct word or phrase above it.

_____ 1. Static, or "white noise," sometimes interferes with a radio or television broadcast.

_____ 2. Noise pollution is unwanted, disturbing, or harmful sounds.

_____ 3. The loudness of heavy traffic can exceed 100 decibels.

_____ 4. People who live near busy urban airports are exposed to noise pollution for less than five hours per day.

_____ 5. High noise levels in factories pose physical and mental problems for workers.

_____ 6. Loud noises make it easy for people to concentrate on what they are doing.

_____ 7. The amplified sound of an average rock concert approaches a loudness of 20 decibels.

_____ 8. You can protect yourself from noise pollution by preventing noise from reaching you and by limiting the loudness of the noise that does reach you.

● _____ 9. People who work with a machine that produces a loudness of 100 decibels should not work at the machine longer than eight hours per day.

● _____ 10. Noise pollution is more of a problem in rural areas than in cities.

During broadcasts and taping sessions, sound technicians monitor the quality of the sound being transmitted.

Acoustical engineers are concerned with the improvement of sound reception and the containment of unwanted sounds. Many work with architects on the design of a building. They recommend materials that will keep sounds from one area out of other areas. Some acoustical engineers specialize in the design of theaters and concert halls. They work to be sure that sounds from the stage can be heard clearly in every section of the audience. Acoustical engineers also work to limit noise pollution in the environment. They design devices that quiet, absorb, and block sounds that disturb nearby residents. Most acoustical engineers work for engineering firms. Some work independently as consultants.

Ultrasound engineers, also called **sonographers,** study the nature of sounds with frequencies above the range of human hearing. Many do research, but some work for industrial and medical equipment companies. Ultrasound engineers often design machinery that is used to diagnose medical problems. They also develop equipment used by manufacturers to measure the thicknesses of various materials or to determine the concentration of particles in paints and solvents. Ultrasound engineers also work on sonar equipment used to locate underwater obstacles.

Sound technicians work in recording studios and in radio and television broadcasting. They make sure that microphones are available and placed to capture sounds from all parts of the studio or stage. During broadcasts and taping sessions, sound technicians monitor the quality of the sound being transmitted and make whatever adjustments are necessary in volume and fidelity. Sound technicians are also employed by theaters in which live plays are performed and by companies that sell audio-visual equipment.

Communications engineers work throughout the communications industry. They design, manufacture, and service a wide variety of communications equipment. Some work in the area of mobile communications. Others work on emergency communications equipment and devices used by those in law enforcement and emergency medicine. Many communications engineers are involved with the development of complete communications systems that serve the needs of particular organizations. Most communications engineers are employed by private companies, but some work in government agencies and departments.

Many employment opportunities exist in the communications field. People with mechanical ability often find work in the service sector of the communications industry. The need for repair and service technicians is always growing. Relatively brief technical training also qualifies a person to operate ultrasound equipment as a diagnostic medical sonographer. During the past few years, the mobile communications field has grown rapidly and offers many opportunities for service technicians and equipment installers. ■

For Further Information

More information about these and related careers is available from the following publications and organizations.

Occupational Outlook Handbook, United States Department of Labor, 1988-1989

A Career in the Telephone Industry, United States Telephone Association

Communications Workers of America
1925 K Street, NW
Washington, DC 20006

American Institute of Architects
1735 New York Avenue
Washington, DC 20006

American Registry of Diagnostic
Medical Sonographers
32 East Hollister Street
Cincinnati, OH 45219

Matter

Chemistry is the study of matter and the changes it undergoes.

Matter

All matter is made of very tiny particles called atoms. Recall that atoms are made of even smaller particles. Electrons have negative electric charges and orbit about the core, or nucleus, of an atom. The protons and the neutrons are located in the nucleus of the atom. Protons have positive electric charges. Neutrons have no electric charge.

You have learned that matter is anything that has mass and occupies space. Gold, water, and cereal are all forms of matter, yet each is obviously different from the others. Matter can be classified, or grouped, in many ways. Some scientists classify matter into two groups: organic matter and inorganic matter. **Organic matter** is any substance that is alive or that came from a once-living organism. Cereal is organic matter. **Inorganic matter** is any substance that is not living. Gold and water are inorganic matter.

Another way to classify matter is by its

physical state. Matter occurs in three physical states: solids, liquids, and gases. Gold and cereal are solids. Water is often a liquid. Ice, however, is the solid state of water. Steam is the gaseous state of water.

Matter can also be classified as elements, compounds, or mixtures. Matter that is made of only one kind of atom is classified as an **element.** Silver, hydrogen, and calcium are only a few of the 109 known elements.

A **compound** is a combination of different kinds of elements in a certain ratio. Water is a compound that is always made of two atoms of hydrogen joined with one atom of oxygen. Table salt is a compound made of one atom of sodium and one atom of chlorine. What are some other common compounds?

A **mixture** is a kind of matter in which the parts composing it are combined in no certain ratios and each part of the mixture keeps its own properties. For example, two bowls of raisin bran poured from the same box probably will not have the same number of raisins. In fact, one box of cereal probably contains different amounts of each ingredient than any other box. Raisin bran is a mixture because each part of the cereal keeps its own properties. You can easily separate the raisins from the bran.

A mixture in which the components are evenly distributed and cannot be easily separated is a **solution.** A cup of black coffee is a solution because the coffee is evenly distributed through the water. When you add milk to the coffee without stirring it, the milk does not mix completely with the coffee. Therefore, that mixture is not a solution until the milk is stirred well into the coffee.

Adding milk to the coffee produces a change in the color of the solution. A **physical change** is a change that does not change the chemical composition of matter. The change in color of the solution from black to brown or beige is a physical change. Physical changes also occur when matter changes state. When water, for example, changes to ice, the change from a liquid to a solid is a physical change. When water is heated to boiling, it physically changes to a gas called steam.

When you burn a log on a campfire, another kind of change takes place. The burning wood turns into a new substance, ash. Ash is chemically different from wood. A substance changes into a new substance during a **chemical change.** The ash cannot be unburned to become wood again. ∎

Lesson Review

In the space provided, write the word or words that best complete each statement.

1. Atoms are made of _____.

2. _____ is matter that is alive or that came from a once-living organism.

3. Gold, cereal, and ice are in the _____ state of matter.

4. Calcium, silver, and hydrogen are _____.

5. A(n) _____ is a kind of matter in which the parts from which it is made are combined in no certain ratios.

6. A mixture in which the components are evenly distributed is a(n) _____.

7. A _____ change does not change the chemical composition of the matter.

8. A substance changes into a new substance during a _____ change.

● 9. Air is made of water vapor and different gases. Air is a(n) _____.

● 10. Carbon dioxide is a gas that is always made of one atom of carbon and two atoms of oxygen. Carbon dioxide is a(n) _____.

Elements

Recall that matter made of only one kind of atom is classified as an element. An element is the simplest form of matter. Elements cannot be broken down by chemical changes. Currently, there are 109 known elements. Of these, 90 occur in nature. The others have been made in laboratories by scientists.

The name of each element can be abbreviated by a **symbol** that consists of one, two, or three letters. The first letter is always capitalized. The symbol for carbon, for example, is C. Hydrogen is abbreviated as H. The symbol for aluminum is Al. Einsteinium, the element named after the scientist Albert Einstein, is abbreviated Es. The symbol for copper, Cu, comes from *cuprum,* the Latin name of the element. Gold is abbreviated Au after *aurum,* its Latin name. Unnilhexium, one of the 19 synthetic elements, is abbreviated Unh.

Recall that all matter can be classified by its physical state. Many elements are solids at room temperature. Copper, silver, and zinc are just a few of these. Other elements, such as hydrogen, oxygen, and helium, are gases at room temperature. Mercury is the only element that is a liquid at room temperature.

What are some other common elements? Iron, a solid element whose symbol is Fe, is important in the human diet. Iron carries oxygen to the blood and builds up a person's resistance to certain diseases. Liver, lean meats, and raisins are good sources of iron. Iron is also mined as an ore.

Gold and silver are other commonly used solid elements. Combined with other elements, gold and silver are used in dentistry, jewelry, some kinds of tableware, and certain coins. Carbon is another very common element. All living organisms contain carbon. Carbon is also the primary element in fossil fuels, such as petroleum, natural gas, and coal.

Carbon has many uses. The soft, black, slippery form of carbon called graphite is used as the "lead" in pencils and as an industrial lubricant. Very fine powdered carbon is used in printer's ink, tires, and some paints. Carbon is added to iron to make steel. The gemstone diamond is a very hard form of carbon.

Silicon, a solid element, and oxygen, a gas, make up nearly three fourths of Earth's crust, or outer layer. Aluminum, iron, calcium, sodium, potassium, magnesium, and several other elements make up the remaining 25 percent. Look at the illustration. What percent of Earth's crust is made of solid elements?

Lead, abbreviated Pb, is a very soft metal. It is used in certain kinds of pipes and tanks because it is not easily corroded. X rays cannot pass through lead. Thus, shields used to protect from exposure to X rays in dentists' and doctors' offices are made of lead.

Hydrogen is a colorless, odorless, and tasteless gas at room temperature. On Earth, hydrogen combines readily with other gases to form compounds. Recall that a compound is a form of matter in which the atoms always combine in a certain ratio. Water is the most common compound on Earth that contains

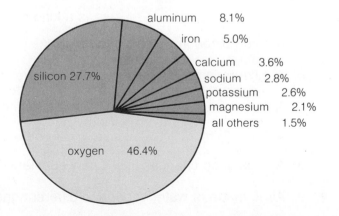

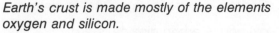

Earth's crust is made mostly of the elements oxygen and silicon.

hydrogen. Two atoms of hydrogen always combine with one atom of oxygen to form water.

Oxygen is another odorless, colorless, tasteless element that makes up about 21 percent of Earth's atmosphere and just over 46 percent of Earth's crust. Oxygen alone won't burn, but it is necessary for combustion.

Oxygen is needed by all living organisms. People and other animals need the oxygen in the air for respiration. A form of oxygen called ozone shields Earth from much of the harmful ultraviolet radiation from the sun.

Most of the known elements do not occur alone. They bond, or are combined, with other elements to produce compounds. Compounds are formed when elements either transfer or share electrons. For example, table salt is formed when sodium, Na, loses an electron to chlorine, Cl, to form sodium chloride, NaCl. **Ionic bonds** are formed when elements transfer electrons. When chlorine, Cl, combines with hydrogen, H, to produce hydrogen chloride, HCl, electrons are shared. **Covalent bonds** form when electrons are shared.

The abbreviation of table salt, NaCl, and of hydrogen chloride, HCl, are chemical formulas. A **chemical formula** is a group of symbols that represent a compound. The most familiar chemical formula is that of water, H_2O. ■

Lesson Review

On the line before each statement, write the letter of the choice that best completes it.

_____ 1. A(n) _____ is the simplest form of matter.

    a. compound   b. chemical   c. element   d. gas

_____ 2. The element gold is represented by the symbol _____.

    a. Au   b. G   c. Go   d . Gol

_____ 3. The elements hydrogen, oxygen, and helium are _____ at room temperature.

    a. solids   b. liquids   c. gases   d. compounds

_____ 4. _____ is an element found in living organisms, fossil fuels, and some paints.

    a. Gold   b. Silver   c. Carbon   d. Silicon

_____ 5. Lead is used in _____.

    a. pencils   b. X-ray shields   c. table salt   d. all of the above

_____ 6. Water is the most common _____ on Earth.

    a. element   b. gas   c. compound   d. solid

_____ 7. A(n) _____ bond forms when elements transfer electrons.

    a. ionic   b. oxidation   c. covalent   d. compound

_____ 8. A(n) _____ bond forms when electrons are shared by elements.

    a. ionic   b. oxidation   c. covalent   d. compound

● _____ 9. CO_2 is a(n) _____.

    a. chemical formula   b. element   c. symbol   d. atom

● _____ 10. Almost _____ percent of Earth's crust is made up of solid elements.

    a. 3   b. 21   c. 55   d. 90

Chemical Reactions

Scientists often refer to the elements as "building blocks" because every substance on Earth is made of one or more elements. Elements can be compared to the building materials used by contractors to construct houses, schools, and other buildings. Some of the same materials, such as brick, wood, and glass, may be used in each building. The amounts of materials used and the way the materials are put together, however, distinguish a house from a school or another building. Contractors use plans and blueprints to show how building materials are arranged and combined to produce a building.

In a similar way, scientists use chemical formulas and equations to represent how elements react in the presence of other elements. Recall that a chemical formula is a group of symbols that represent a compound. For example, glucose, a simple form of sugar, and formaldehyde, a poisonous gas, are both made of carbon, hydrogen, and oxygen. The chemical formula of glucose is $C_6H_{12}O_6$ and that of formaldehyde is CH_2O. There are six atoms of carbon, 12 atoms of hydrogen, and six atoms of oxygen in one molecule of glucose. How many atoms of hydrogen are in a molecule of formaldehyde?

A chemical formula simply lists the elements that make up a compound. What happens when elements combine to form compounds? A **chemical equation** represents the changes that occur during a chemical reaction. For example, when iron combines with sulfur, iron sulfide is produced. The chemical equation for this reaction is:

$$Fe + S \rightarrow FeS.$$

The equation is read: "one atom of iron reacts with one atom of sulfur to produce one molecule of iron sulfide." Substances on the left side of a chemical equation are the **reactants.** The substances on the right side of the equation are the **products.**

You are very familiar with the chemical formula for water, H_2O. How does water form? Water forms when hydrogen combines with oxygen as in the equation:

$$2H_2 + O_2 \rightarrow 2H_2O.$$

Like all mathematical equations, chemical equations must be balanced. The number of each kind of atom must be the same on each side of the equation. When water forms, four atoms of hydrogen combine with two atoms of oxygen. The number "2" in front of the hydrogen on the left side of the equation is a **coefficient,** a number that serves to show the amount of a substance needed in a chemical equation. The subscript "2" on both the hydrogen and the oxygen indicates that two atoms of each are needed to form a molecule of each element. By multiplying the coefficient by the number of atoms on both sides of the

Combustion is a chemical reaction that produces light and heat.

equation, you can determine whether or not the equation is balanced. Notice that there are four atoms of hydrogen on each side of the equation and two atoms of oxygen.

Elements can combine with one another in many ways. Scientists classify chemical reactions into three kinds: synthesis, decomposition, and displacement. **Synthesis** occurs when two or more elements or compounds synthesize, or join, to form one new compound. The formation of iron sulfide and the formation of water are both synthesis reactions.

Decomposition occurs when a substance breaks down into one or more other substances. For example, if table sugar is heated, it decomposes, or breaks down, into carbon and

water. Decomposition reactions are the reverse of synthesis reactions.

A reaction in which one or more elements displace other elements from a compound is a **displacement reaction.** For example, when sodium bicarbonate, Na_2CO_3, is added to water containing calcium sulfate, $CaSO_4$, the water is softened because the calcium is removed. The equation for this displacement reaction is:

$$Na_2CO_3 + CaSO_4 \rightarrow Na_2SO_4 + CaCO_3.$$

Notice that the sodium displaced the calcium in the calcium sulfate. Also, the calcium displaced the sodium in the sodium bicarbonate. This type of reaction is called a double displacement reaction. ■

Lesson Review

Determine whether each of the following statements is true or false. Correct the false statements by crossing out the word or phrase that makes it false and by writing the correct word or phrase above it.

_____ 1. Chemical formulas and equations are used to represent how elements react in the presence of other elements.

_____ 2. The chemical formula for table sugar, or glucose, is $C_7H_{12}O_6$.

_____ 3. A chemical formula represents the changes that occur during a chemical reaction.

_____ 4. Substances on the left side of a chemical equation are the reactants.

_____ 5. In order to balance, the number of each kind of atom must be different on each side of a chemical equation.

_____ 6. Water forms when two atoms of hydrogen combine with two atoms of oxygen.

_____ 7. Synthesis occurs when two or more elements or compounds join to form one new compound.

_____ 8. When table sugar is heated, it decomposes into carbon and water.

● _____ 9. $Fe_2O_3 + 3CO \rightarrow 2Fe + 3CO_2$ is not a balanced equation.

● _____ 10. The formation of carbon dioxide, CO_2, from carbon, C, and oxygen, O_2, is a synthesis reaction.

The Periodic Table

The English chemist J. R. Newlands investigated the properties of the elements that were known in the mid-1800s. As he did this, he noticed a pattern in the atomic structure of elements with similar chemical properties. This discovery led him to conclude that elements could be grouped according to their similarities. At about the same time, Lothar Meyer, a German chemist, proposed a table that listed the elements known at the time in much the same order as Newlands had determined.

Dmitri Mendeleev, a Russian chemist, is given much of the credit for the present periodic table of elements. The **periodic table** is a table that classifies the known elements according to their properties. In 1869, Mendeleev arranged the 63 elements known at that time into a table according to their properties. Mendeleev left some blank spaces in the table. He believed that they would be filled by elements that were not yet discovered. In fact, he was able to predict the properties of these unknown elements by the patterns that existed in his table. Many of the 46 elements that have been discovered since Mendeleev's time were discovered based on his predictions.

Elements in the periodic table are arranged in groups and periods. A **group** is a vertical column that contains elements with similar properties. For example, Group IB contains copper, whose symbol is Cu, silver, Ag, and gold, Au. A **period** is a horizontal row of the the periodic table. Period 3 contains the elements sodium, magnesium, aluminum, silicon, phosphorous, sulfur, chlorine, and argon. Elements in a period are listed in order of increasing atomic number. **Atomic number** is the number of protons in the nucleus of an atom. The atomic number of copper is 29. What is the atomic number of gold?

The elements in Group IA, except for hydrogen, which is in a class by itself, are called alkali metals. In general, these elements are shiny and are good conductors of heat and electrical current. Lithium, sodium, potassium, and the other three elements of the group are used in manufacturing processes.

Group IIA contains the alkaline earth metals. These elements are not as reactive as those in Group IA and are often found combined with other elements. Beryllium is a fairly rare element. Magnesium is used in aircraft because it is strong but lightweight. Calcium is used in construction and agriculture and is also important for healthy bones and teeth. The other elements of Group IIA— strontium, barium, and radium—are radioactive.

Elements belonging to Groups IIIA through IIB are called transition elements. All the transition elements are metals. Metals are elements that are good conductors of heat and electricity. Metals also are generally shiny and relatively hard substances. You are probably familiar with many of the transition elements. Recall that iron, Fe, is important in the human diet. It is also used in many manufacturing processes. Nickel is used in the five-cent coin of the United States. Copper is used in electrical wiring. Recall that gold and silver are used in dentistry and jewelry. Zinc compounds are used in certain kinds of paint and in some medicines. Mercury, Hg, is used in thermometers.

Group IIIB, also called the boron group, contains boron, aluminum, gallium, indium, and thallium. Boron is used in water softeners. Aluminum is a good conductor of heat and electricity. It is used in pots and pans, some electrical wiring, foils, and in certain types of medicine. The remaining three elements in this group are used in electronic devices.

A Periodic Table of the Elements

Legend:
- atomic number — 12
- symbol of element — **Mg**
- element name — Magnesium

Elements above and to the right of this line are nonmetals.

Elements below and to the left of this line are metals.

Elements in this column are noble gases.

periods / groups	IA	IIA	IIIA	IVA	VA	VIA	VIIA	VIIIB			IB	IIB	IIIB	IVB	VB	VIB	VIIB	VIIIB
1	1 H Hydrogen																	2 He Helium
2	3 Li Lithium	4 Be Beryllium											5 B Boron	6 C Carbon	7 N Nitrogen	8 O Oxygen	9 F Fluorine	10 Ne Neon
3	11 Na Sodium	12 Mg Magnesium											13 Al Aluminum	14 Si Silicon	15 P Phosphorus	16 S Sulfur	17 Cl Chlorine	18 Ar Argon
4	19 K Potassium	20 Ca Calcium	21 Sc Scandium	22 Ti Titanium	23 V Vanadium	24 Cr Chromium	25 Mn Manganese	26 Fe Iron	27 Co Cobalt	28 Ni Nickel	29 Cu Copper	30 Zn Zinc	31 Ga Gallium	32 Ge Germanium	33 As Arsenic	34 Se Selenium	35 Br Bromine	36 Kr Krypton
5	37 Rb Rubidium	38 Sr Strontium	39 Y Yttrium	40 Zr Zirconium	41 Nb Niobium	42 Mo Molybdenum	43 Tc Technetium	44 Ru Ruthenium	45 Rh Rhodium	46 Pd Palladium	47 Ag Silver	48 Cd Cadmium	49 In Indium	50 Sn Tin	51 Sb Antimony	52 Te Tellurium	53 I Iodine	54 Xe Xenon
6	55 Cs Cesium	56 Ba Barium	57—71* See Below	72 Hf Hafnium	73 Ta Tantalum	74 W Tungsten	75 Re Rhenium	76 Os Osmium	77 Ir Iridium	78 Pt Platinum	79 Au Gold	80 Hg Mercury	81 Tl Thallium	82 Pb Lead	83 Bi Bismuth	84 Po Polonium	85 At Astatine	86 Rn Radon
7	87 Fr Francium	88 Ra Radium	89—103** See Below	104 (unnamed)	105 (unnamed)	106 (unnamed)	107 (unnamed)	108 (unnamed)	109 (unnamed)									

*Lanthanide series

57 La Lanthanum	58 Ce Cerium	59 Pr Praseodymium	60 Nd Neodymium	61 Pm Promethium	62 Sm Samarium	63 Eu Europium	64 Gd Gadolinium	65 Tb Terbium	66 Dy Dysprosium	67 Ho Holmium	68 Er Erbium	69 Tm Thulium	70 Yb Ytterbium	71 Lu Lutetium

**Actinide series

89 Ac Actinium	90 Th Thorium	91 Pa Protactinium	92 U Uranium	93 Np Neptunium	94 Pu Plutonium	95 Am Americium	96 Cm Curium	97 Bk Berkelium	98 Cf Californium	99 Es Einsteinium	100 Fm Fermium	101 Md Mendelevium	102 No Nobelium	103 Lr Lawrencium

Recall that carbon is found in all living organisms. In fact, it is the second most common element in your body. Elements in the carbon group, or Group IVB, are non-metals. Most nonmetals are poor conductors of electricity and heat. Silicon is used in most communications equipment and as an abrasive. Tin is used to make some fabrics flame resistant. Until recently, lead was commonly used in paints and gasolines. The use of lead in such products has been reduced due to its high toxicity.

Elements in Group VB are not very reactive. Nitrogen, N, is a gas at room temperature. Three fourths of Earth's atmosphere is nitrogen. Nitrogen is needed by all living organisms. Phosphorous, whose symbol is P, together with nitrogen, is used in many fertilizers. One member of the nitrogen group, arsenic, is poisonous.

The elements in the oxygen group, or Group VIB, combine easily with other elements to form compounds with covalent bonds. Recall that covalent bonds form when electrons are shared. Oxygen is a gas that makes up about 21 percent of Earth's atmosphere. It combines readily with other elements to form compounds called oxides. Sulfur is used in medicines, fertilizers, and rubber, among many other products.

The halogens, or salt makers, make up Group VIIB. Fluoride salts are added to drinking water to prevent tooth decay. Recall that when sodium combines with chlorine, common table salt is formed. Iodine is important to the human diet and is often added to table salt. Astatine is the only radioactive element in Group VIIB.

Group VIII is called the noble gases. Like the nobles of long ago who didn't associate with the common people, these gases do not combine easily with other elements. Helium is lighter than air and is used to keep balloons afloat. Helium, neon, and argon are used to make certain kinds of signs. Krypton is used in fluorescent lights. Xenon can be used in photography. Radon is a radioactive element that is used to treat some kinds of cancer. ■

Lesson Review

In the space provided, write the word or words that best complete each statement.

1. _____ is given much of the credit for the present periodic table.

2. The periodic table classifies elements according to their _____.

3. A _____ is a vertical column on the periodic table that contains elements with similar properties.

4. A _____ is a horizontal row of the periodic table.

5. The number of protons in an atom is the atom's _____.

6. Copper, zinc, gold, silver, and mercury are _____ elements.

7. Group IIIB is also called the _____ group.

8. Nitrogen and phosphorous belong to Group VB and are used in _____.

● 9. Palladium is a(n) _____ element that belongs to the _____ period.

● 10. The atomic number of krypton is _____.

Environmental Pollution

Advances in chemistry have helped to eliminate certain diseases, to increase crop yields, to improve certain kinds of fabrics, and to make more fuel-efficient forms of transportation. These improvements are only a few of the many thousands of positive results of chemical research. And, as with most scientific achievements, along with the benefits of the advances made in chemistry come negative effects.

One of the most serious problems facing the world today is environmental pollution. How clean is the air you breathe? Is your water safe to drink? What kinds of chemicals does your food contain? How does environmental pollution affect the plants and animals, including humans, on planet Earth?

Air pollution is the introduction of harmful substances into the air. Some air pollution is the result of activities in nature. Erupting volcanoes and natural forest fires are just two sources of air pollution not caused by people. However, most air pollution today is the result of human activities. The burning of fossil fuels such as oil, coal, gasoline, and diesel fuel, along with the burning of trash and garbage, adds hundreds of millions of tons of harmful substances to Earth's atmosphere each year.

Most air pollutants are either solids or gases. **Particulates** are tiny pieces of solids that are added to the air when substances are burned. Dust, ashes, and soot are particulates. Plowing, construction, and mining also add solid matter to air. What are some other sources of particulates?

Motor vehicles, airplanes, and factories add gases such as nitric oxide, carbon dioxide, and sulfur dioxide to the air when they burn oil, natural gas, and coal. **Smog** is a kind of air pollution that forms when a chemical reaction occurs among sunlight, nitric oxide, sulfur dioxide, and compounds containing carbon and hydrogen.

When sulfur dioxide combines with moisture in the air, sulfuric acid forms. When this acid falls to Earth with rain or snow, it is called **acid rain.** Acid rain damages buildings and corrodes certain kinds of metals. In parts of the United States, Canada, and Germany, acid rain has killed large numbers of trees in many forests. When added to rivers and lakes, this precipitation changes the acidity of the water and may kill fish, plants, and other forms of aquatic life. Acid rain can also reduce the yields of many crops.

Fluorocarbons, a group of gases used in propellants and as coolants, are another source of air pollution. These compounds break down a form of oxygen called ozone. The **ozone layer** is a layer of gas that protects Earth and its inhabitants from harmful ultraviolet radiation from the sun. Without the ozone layer, life as we know it on Earth isn't possible.

Water pollution is another form of environmental pollution due in part to the advances made in chemical research. In addition to acid rain, bodies of water are being polluted by chemical wastes from factories. Some factories, despite certain regulations, discharge their industrial wastes into nearby bodies of water. These wastes often cause the aquatic life in the lakes and rivers to die.

Thermal pollution is another form of water pollution, caused when factories or power plants discharge heated water into local bodies of water. Sometimes the heated water kills the aquatic life immediately. In other cases, the increase in temperature causes certain algae to grow and overpopulate the water. This causes a decrease in the oxygen needed by

This photograph shows a blanket of smog hanging over Denver, Colorado. Smog forms when a chemical reaction occurs among sunlight, nitric oxide, sulfur dioxide, and compounds containing carbon and hydrogen.

the other life forms in the water, causing them to die.

Fertilizers and pesticides have greatly increased the amounts and kinds of crops grown in this country and around the world. When carried away by water that runs off the land, however, they pollute streams, rivers, lakes, and ground water. This form of pollution makes drinking water for farm animals and people unsafe. Fertilizers and pesticides also harm or even destroy certain bacteria and other organisms that are beneficial to crops.

How many things do you own or use every day that are made, at least in part, from plastic? The list is probably long. Hair dryers, kitchen appliances, some fast-food containers, and certain parts of your car's interior are only a few of the hundreds of thousands of everyday items made of plastic. Many plastics are lightweight yet durable. Plastics have probably made your life very convenient in many ways. Yet plastics are a major part of the solid wastes that pollute the environment. Most plastics are nondegradable. That is, they are unable to be broken down into substances that don't pollute the air, water, and soil. Those plastics that do degrade, or break down, often break down into harmful substances that pollute the water and soil. Burning plastics pollutes the air.

What can you do to reduce environmental pollution? Car-pooling, using fuel-efficient cars or public transportation, and walking or bicycling to your destination help to reduce air pollution. Using products that don't pollute the environment is another part of the solution. Certain laundry detergents and soaps contain little or no phosphates, which are compounds that contribute to water pollution. Rather than having your groceries packed in plastic bags, choose paper bags. You can also make every effort to recycle items that can be reprocessed and used again. Items such as newspapers and aluminum cans can be made into new newsprint and new cans. What other materials can you recycle? ∎

Lesson Review

On the line before each statement, write the letter of the choice that best completes the statement.

_____ 1. Advances in chemistry have _____.

    a. contributed to environmental pollution

    b. increased crop yields

    c. improved certain kinds of fabrics

    d. all of the above

_____ 2. _____ pollution is the introduction of harmful substances into the atmosphere.

    a. Air   b. Thermal   c. Degradable   d. Water

_____ 3. Fossil fuels include _____.

    a. gasoline   b. oil   c. coal   d. all of the above

_____ 4. _____ forms when sunlight reacts with nitric oxide, sulfur dioxide, and compounds containing carbon and hydrogen.

    a. Acid rain   b. Smog   c. Particulate   d. Ozone

_____ 5. _____ has killed many plants and animals in this country and in other countries.

    a. Ozone   b. Fluorocarbon   c. Acid rain   d. None of the above

_____ 6. The gas that protects Earth from harmful ultraviolet radiation is _____.

    a. carbon dioxide   b. nitric oxide   c. sulfur dioxide   d. ozone

_____ 7. _____ pollution occurs when heated water is released into lakes and rivers.

    a. Thermal   b. Air   c. Ozone   d. Degradable

_____ 8. Plastics contribute to _____ pollution.

    a. water   b. soil   c. air   d. all of the above

● _____ 9. Burning trash mainly pollutes _____.

    a. water bodies   b. the air   c. soil   d. none of the above

● _____ 10. _____ are materials that can be recycled.

    a. Aluminum cans   b. Newspapers   c. Glass bottles   d. All of the above

Chemistry teachers prepare and give lectures and also conduct laboratory sessions.

Chemists are scientists who study matter and how it reacts to form other kinds of matter. Most chemists work in research and development. These chemists may spend time in an office doing theoretical research or in a laboratory conducting experiments to develop new and better fibers, drugs, or other products. The work of a chemist may take him or her inside chemical plants or outdoors to gather samples of water, soil, or air to analyze back at the laboratory for pollutants. Most chemists work for private industries.

Chemistry teachers assist students to help them learn the basic principles of chemistry. Chemistry teachers usually work in high schools, technical schools, community and junior colleges, and universities. Chemistry teachers prepare and give lectures. They also conduct laboratory sessions during which they help students develop lab skills and increase their knowledge of chemistry. Along with a strong knowledge of chemistry, these teachers must have a good general science background.

Chemistry literature specialists are people who can communicate their knowledge of chemistry to others. Chemistry literature specialists can be employed as librarians, writers, and editors. Librarians catalogue and distribute many kinds of literature, including chemistry books, journals, and magazines. Writers may work for chemical companies as well as for newspaper, magazine, and textbook publishers. Writers who work in industry often inform the public about the company itself, new products, and advances in chemical science. Writers who work with publishers assist editors with the writing and publication of chemical literature.

Chemistry laboratory technicians assist chemists who work in labs. These technicians conduct routine chemical experiments, record data, and follow procedures outlined by the chemists who supervise them. Often these assistants test the chemical properties of new products. In addition to their scientific work, most technicians are also responsible for maintaining a clean and safe laboratory.

Chemical sales representatives sell chemical products for various kinds of companies. "Sales reps," as they are often called, demonstrate the use of products and help customers determine the types and amounts of products needed. Most chemical sales representatives are employed by pharmaceutical companies.

A wide variety of opportunities exists for those who have a background in high school chemistry along with some additional training. Skilled workers are needed throughout the chemical industry. On-the-job experience can frequently lead to a technical position. Career opportunities also exist in state and federal agencies that are responsible for monitoring the condition of the environment. ■

For Further Information

More information about these and related careers is available from the following publications and organizations.

Chemical Technology, American Chemical Society

Journal of Technical Writing and Communications, Baywood Publishing Company

American Chemical Society
Career Services
16th Street, NW
Washington, DC 20036

Manufacturers' Agents
National Association
P.O. Box 16878
Irvine, CA 92713

National Education Association
1201 16th Street, NW
Washington, DC 20036

Radioactivity

The generators in this electric utility plant are powered by a nuclear reactor.

Radiation and Radioactivity

Many of the 109 known elements have more than one form. The different forms of an element are called **isotopes.** Isotopes of a certain element contain different numbers of neutrons. The element uranium, for example, has several isotopes. The atomic number of uranium, or U, is 92. Recall that the atomic number is the number of protons in the nucleus of an atom. **Mass number** is the number of protons and neutrons in the nucleus of an atom. The mass number of one type of uranium isotope is 238. Therefore, this isotope, called U-238, has 146 neutrons in its nucleus. The mass number of another uranium isotope is 234. How many neutrons are in its nucleus?

As you have learned, elements are made of atoms. Atoms, in turn, are made of protons, neutrons, and electrons. Electrons

orbit the nucleus of the atom. The nucleus contains the protons and neutrons. Scientists have discovered that not all nuclei are stable. The nuclei of some unstable elements, such as uranium, give off charged particles, or radiation, during a process called **radioactive decay.**

There are three kinds of radiation released when radioactive elements decay, or decompose. **Alpha particles** are made of two neutrons and two protons. They have a positive electric charge and are identical to a helium nucleus. The element helium is a gas with the atomic number 2. High-energy alpha particles are given off, but they rapidly lose energy when they strike matter. Alpha particles have very little penetration power.

Beta particles are electrons that travel near the speed of light. The radioactive nuclei of some atoms emit particles with negative electric charges. Other atoms, however, give off positively-charged particles called positrons. Beta particles can penetrate matter much better than alpha particles. Some beta particles can penetrate wood to a depth of about half an inch.

Gamma rays are forms of high-energy radiation that have no electric charge. Gamma rays have short wavelengths and travel at the speed of light. They can penetrate most matter far more deeply than beta particles. Gamma rays can penetrate iron that is over an inch thick. In large amounts, gamma rays can be harmful to human tissues and organs because they can penetrate these substances very easily.

All radioactive elements decay at a certain rate called a half-life. A **half-life** is the time needed for half of the atoms in a radioactive element to decay. The half-lives of radioactive materials range from a fraction of a second to billions of years. For example, the half-life of polonium-214 is 0.001 seconds. Carbon-14 has a half-life of 5,730 years. The isotope uranium-238 has a half-life of 4.5 billion years. How much of a ten-pound sample of carbon-14 would be left after one half-life? ■

Lesson Review

On the line before each statement, write the letter of the choice that best completes each statement.

_____ 1. Isotopes of the same element contain different numbers of _____.

    a. protons   b. neutrons   c. positrons   d. electrons

_____ 2. _____ is the number of protons and neutrons in the nucleus of an atom.

    a. Atomic number   b. Radiation number   c. Mass number   d. Gamma number

_____ 3. Unstable atoms give off _____ during radioactive decay.

    a. radiation   b. isotopes   c. carbon-14   d. all of the above

_____ 4. _____ are made of two neutrons and two protons.

    a. Alpha particles   b. Gamma rays   c. Beta particles   d. Half-life rays

_____ 5. Electrons that travel near the speed of light are _____.

    a. alpha particles   b. gamma rays   c. beta particles   d. neutrons

_____ 6. High-energy radiation with no electric charge is a(n) _____.

    a. alpha particle   b. gamma ray   c. beta particle   d. positron

_____ 7. _____ can penetrate iron that is over an inch thick.

    a. Isotopes   b. Beta particles   c. Alpha particles   d. Gamma rays

_____ 8. The time needed for half of a radioactive material to decay is the _____.

    a. atomic number   b. mass number   c. half-life   d. none of the above

● _____ 9. There are 92 protons and _____ neutrons in uranium-234.

    a. 142   b. 146   c. 234   d. 238

● _____ 10. The nucleus of a *stable* element probably _____.

    a. gives off alpha particles   c. gives off gamma rays

    b. gives off beta particles   d. gives off no radiation

Detecting Radioactivity

Although radiation can't be seen or felt, scientists can detect and measure the radio-activity of a substance. The most commonly used radiation detectors are cloud chambers, bubble chambers, and Geiger counters.

The **cloud chamber,** which was developed in 1912 by the British physicist Charles T. R. Wilson, is a device that makes it possible to see the paths made by electrically charged atomic particles. A simple cloud chamber is a container fitted with a piston. The containers of most cloud chambers are filled with supersaturated air. **Supersaturated air** is air that contains more water vapor than usual at a given temperature.

When electrically-charged particles such as alpha or beta particles pass through a cloud chamber, they react with the atoms that make up the air to produce visible streaks. The streaks disappear almost at once but can be photographed with special film before they fade from view. The streaks produced by alpha particles are thicker and shorter than those produced by beta particles. Could gamma rays be detected in cloud chambers? Why or why not?

Another device for detecting radiation was invented by Donald A. Glaser, an American physicist, in 1953. A **bubble chamber** is a tightly sealed metal box with a viewing window. The container is filled with a very hot liquid that is under great pressure. Propane or liquid hydrogen is commonly used in bubble chambers because they can be heated precisely.

For a bubble chamber to be able to detect radiation, the liquid in the chamber is heated to a temperature just below its boiling point. When the liquid reaches this temperature, atomic particles are shot into the chamber. These particles cause the liquid to boil as they pass through it. Bubbles are formed along the paths of the particles. The bubble tracks are then quickly photographed with especially fast film through the viewing window. The photographs of the bubble tracks allow scientists to measure the mass of the particle making the bubble and to determine the electric charge of the particle.

A **Geiger counter,** also called a Geiger-Müller counter after the two German physicists who invented it, is a device that detects radiation by the formation of an electric current. In a Geiger counter, a fine wire is stretched along the length of a metal tube containing a gas. The wire and the walls of the tube serve as electrodes, which are conductors used to establish an electrical contact with a nonmetallic part of a circuit.

The electric current keeps the wire in a Geiger counter charged at a level of about 1,000

This machine uses tracers to test the thickness of sheets of steel coming off a strip mill.

volts. This creates an electric field near the wire. Alpha and beta particles from the radioactive material collide with atoms that make up the gas. Electrons are released and move along the wire to produce an electric pulse. The pulse is amplified and counted by a meter in the Geiger counter.

Geiger counters can detect the presence of alpha particles, beta particles, and gamma rays. These detection devices are used to locate uranium and other radioactive elements. Geiger counters can also be used to detect levels of radiation in the vicinity of nuclear reactors. Geiger counters are found in the control rooms of all nuclear power plants.

While they are not a mechanical device for determining the presence or level of radiation, tracers can be used to show the paths made by radioactive materials. **Tracers** are radioactive isotopes that can be used to follow a biological or mechanical process. For example, tracers are used to track the path of petroleum through a pipeline. Tracers can also be used to tag animals in order to study their migration patterns. You are probably familiar with the use of tracers in medicine. They can be used to study blood circulation and the progress of a substance that has been injected into the human body. Tracers have made it possible to track things whose progress could only be guessed at before. ■

Lesson Review

Determine whether each of the following statements is true or false. Correct the false statements by crossing out the word or phrase that makes it false and by writing the correct word or phrase above it.

_____ 1. Radiation can be seen and felt.

_____ 2. Most cloud chambers are filled with supersaturated air.

_____ 3. A bubble chamber makes it possible to see alpha or beta particles because they react with air to produce streaks.

_____ 4. A bubble chamber is a tightly sealed metal box with a viewing window.

_____ 5. The liquid in a bubble chamber is heated to just below boiling before atomic particles are shot into the chamber.

_____ 6. Bubble chambers allow scientists to determine the mass of the particle that makes the bubble as well as its charge.

_____ 7. A Geiger counter detects radiation by the formation of an electric current.

_____ 8. In a Geiger counter, protons are moved along the wire to produce an electric pulse.

• _____ 9. Geiger counters can be used to study the feeding habits of fish.

• _____ 10. Gamma rays cannot be detected in a cloud chamber.

Fission and Fusion

As you recall, the nucleus, or core, of an atom is made of protons and neutrons. Very strong forces hold these subatomic particles together. In unstable atoms, however, the forces are not strong enough to keep the protons and neutrons in place. When these unstable atoms decay, tremendous amounts of energy are released. Nuclear energy is the energy released when changes take place in the nucleus of an atom. There are two kinds of nuclear reactions: fission and fusion.

Nuclear fission occurs when a heavy radioactive nucleus splits to form two new nuclei. Elements with atomic numbers greater than 90 can undergo nuclear fission. Some of these elements can fission spontaneously. Others fission only when they are hit by

The device shown in this photograph has been used in nuclear fusion experiments.

particles such as neutrons. For example, one isotope of uranium, U-235, undergoes fission when it is bombarded by neutrons. The bombardment causes the uranium-235 nucleus to split into two new nuclei. Neutrons are also products of fission reactions.

In some cases, barium and krypton are formed when U-235 fissions. Other products of the fission of U-235 are rubidium and cesium, or zinc and samarium. In all fission reactions of U-235, the mass of the products is less than the mass of the reactants. According to the law of conservation of mass, mass can be neither created nor destroyed. What happens to the "missing" mass?

Albert Einstein, a German physicist, discovered the relationship between energy and mass. The famous equation, $E = mc^2$, states that energy, E, equals the mass of an object, m, times the speed of light squared, c^2. The "missing" mass changes to energy during the process of fission.

Due to the vast amounts of energy released during fission, certain elements that undergo fission are used as fuel in nuclear reactors. Uranium is used in many reactors because when it undergoes fission, a continuous series of fission reactions often occurs. The neutrons that are produced can react with other nuclei of uranium and cause them to split. As more and more neutrons are released, there are more fission reactions. This continuous series of fission reactions is called a **nuclear chain reaction.** A nuclear chain reaction is similar in principle to a falling row of dominoes. When the first domino is pushed, it topples onto the second domino, which topples onto the third, and so on until the last domino falls.

Billions of atoms undergo fission in a fraction of a second. If fission occurs as an uncontrolled nuclear reaction, a tremendous atomic explosion can take place. The atomic bomb gets its destructive force from an uncontrolled chain reaction. Temperatures produced during an explosion can exceed ten million degrees Celsius. This intense heat is accompanied by shock waves and extremely dangerous amounts of radiation.

Nuclear fusion is a reaction that occurs when two nuclei fuse, or combine, to form one heavier nucleus. The majority of scientists believe that the temperatures necessary for fusion to occur are extremely high, approaching millions of degrees Celsius. In 1989, however, two scientists from Utah claimed that they had caused fusion at room temperature. The scientific community is continuing to investigate this claim.

Many fusion reactions occur in stars where temperatures exceed 20 million degrees C.

For example, four nuclei of hydrogen fuse to form one helium nucleus. Carbon, oxygen, and silicon also form during fusion reactions in stars. During all fusion reactions, some of the mass is changed to energy.

Because of the difficulty of generating temperatures needed for fusion, all of the nuclear energy used today is made available through fission. The major problem with fission, in addition to its high cost at present, is the difficulty of disposing of the radioactive wastes that result. Many of the products of fission are radioactive elements with long half-lives. How to dispose of these substances so that they do not harm people or contaminate the environment is an ongoing problem yet to be solved. ■

Lesson Review

In the space before each number, write the letter of the word or group of words in Column 2 that matches the description in Column 1.

Column 1

_____ 1. the nucleus of an atom is made of neutrons and these subatomic particles

_____ 2. occurs when heavy nuclei split in two

_____ 3. used to bombard U-235 in nuclear fission

_____ 4. one of the new elements formed from the fission of U-235

_____ 5. mass is converted to this in a nuclear reaction

_____ 6. a series of continuous fission reactions

_____ 7. an example of an uncontrolled nuclear reaction

_____ 8. reaction that occurs when atoms are fused to form a new nucleus

● _____ 9. fusion occurs here

● _____ 10. what rubidium and cesium are

Column 2

a. atomic bomb

b. barium

c. chain reaction

d. energy

e. fission

f. fusion

g. neutrons

h. protons

i. radioactive wastes

j. the sun

Nuclear Reactors

Nuclear energy is made usable by a device called a nuclear reactor. A **nuclear reactor** makes it possible to control the process of nuclear fission and to use the energy generated from the reaction. The energy produced from fission is converted to thermal energy, which, in turn, is converted to steam. The steam is used to run turbines that generate power.

Today, most nuclear reactors in the world are used to generate electricity. These reactors differ in size and design, but most of them have five basic parts: a core, a moderator, control rods, a coolant, and a pressure vessel. In addition to these basic parts, nuclear reactors have safety systems that protect both the people who operate them and the people who live near them.

The central part of a nuclear reactor is the **core.** The core contains the nuclear fuel, which is uranium oxide pellets. Fission of the uranium nuclei causes a chain reaction during which millions of uranium atoms split within a fraction of a second. This process changes small amounts of mass into vast amounts of energy.

The **moderator** in a nuclear reactor is a substance, usually water, that slows down the neutrons formed during fission. Slowing these particles down increases the likelihood that fission will continue. Without a moderator, the chain reaction needed to provide energy might not occur.

Control rods regulate the speed of the chain reaction in a nuclear reactor. The rods are made of metals such as cadmium or boron that can absorb the neutrons released. When the reactor core is loaded with fuel, the control rods are withdrawn slightly from the core so that they don't absorb too many neutrons. When the rods are in this position, the chain reaction can begin. Once the reaction has begun, the rods are partially inserted into the core to slow the chain reaction.

The purpose of the **coolant** in a nuclear reactor is to remove thermal energy from the reactor. The coolant also controls the temperature of the reactor core and prevents it from overheating. Various gases and liquids are used as coolants in most reactors. Water is a common coolant used in nuclear reactors.

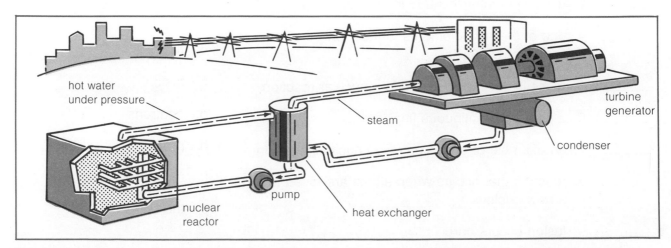

hot water under pressure

nuclear reactor

pump

heat exchanger

steam

turbine generator

condenser

This illustration shows the main parts of a nuclear reactor that supply energy in an electric power plant.

The **pressure vessel** of a nuclear reactor encases the core and contains channels through which the coolant flows. The thick, metal walls of the vessel are designed to withstand the tremendous pressures created during a fission chain reaction.

Every nuclear reactor has a safety system designed to prevent accidents. All safety systems contain **safety shields** made of thick concrete that surround the reactor's pressure vessel. The concrete absorbs the radiation that is emitted from the core of the reactor. Sensitive instruments that measure the level of radiation around the shields are used to ensure that no leaks occur.

Various other devices guard against accidents in a nuclear reactor. Every reactor has a set of safety rods that can be inserted into the core if the rate of fission increases too quickly. Reactors also have an emergency cooling system that will keep the temperature of the core at a safe level if the reactor's coolant is lost. This emergency cooling system would flood the core with water in the event of overheating.

The most serious problem associated with nuclear reactors is the possibility of meltdown. **Meltdown** is a condition that could take place if, in the absence of coolant, the core got so hot that it could burn the floor of the building that housed the reactor. This melting could continue deep into Earth's crust. During a meltdown, considerable amounts of radiation could be released into Earth's atmosphere. In 1979, a series of mechanical failures and human errors almost caused a meltdown at the Three Mile Island nuclear power plant in Pennsylvania. More recently, in 1986, a partial meltdown did occur in the Soviet Union. The full extent of this disaster is still not clear. ■

Lesson Review

In the space provided, write the word or words that best complete each statement.

1. A(n) _____ makes it possible to control the process of fission and to use the energy generated from the reaction.

2. Most of the nuclear reactors in the world today are used to generate _____ .

3. The fission chain reaction takes place in the _____ of a nuclear reactor.

4. The _____ increases the likelihood that fission will continue.

5. The speed of a chain reaction in a reactor is controlled by the _____.

6. Many reactors use _____ as a coolant to prevent them from overheating.

7. The _____ encases the core and contains the channels through which the coolant flows in a nuclear reactor.

8. _____ could occur if, in the absence of coolant, the reactor overheats.

● 9. The full extent of the partial meltdown in the Soviet Union remains unclear because there is no way to measure the amount of _____ released into the Earth's atmosphere.

● 10. If the control rods are completely _____ into the core, fission stops.

Nuclear Energy

At the present time, there are about 500 nuclear reactors in use throughout the world. Nuclear reactors produce vast amounts of energy from small amounts of fuel. Reactors are also a clean source of energy. That is, they do not pollute the air like the burning of coal and oil does. Cooling towers at nuclear power plants prevent thermal pollution. Recall that thermal pollution occurs when hot industrial wastewaters are released into nearby bodies of water.

As with most forms of energy, there are also disadvantages to using nuclear energy. The release of nuclear radiation into the environment is the greatest danger associated with nuclear fission. Recall that radiation is produced by nuclear reactions in the form of alpha particles, beta particles, and gamma rays. In large doses, gamma rays are very dangerous to living organisms. Like X rays, they can penetrate living tissue and cause changes in the atoms that make up the tissues. These changes can damage and even kill the tissue. Small amounts of radiation can cause cancer. Exposure to significant amounts of radiation leads to death within a few months of exposure.

Because of the danger of radiation leakage, nuclear reactors are equipped with many safety systems. Yet, accidents can and have taken place. The worst nuclear accident to date happened in a power plant located in Chernobyl, a small town in the Soviet Union. In April of 1986, workers at the plant conducted a test of the reactor's emergency systems without the consent or knowledge of the supervisors of the plant. In order to make the test, the operators shut down the reactor's emergency cooling system. At the same time, they turned off another control system designed to automatically shut down the reactor if the rate of fission increased too rapidly.

When the systems were shut off, the reactor's power dropped to only one percent of its capacity. At this point in the test, the workers removed the control rods from the reactor's core. Control rods regulate the speed of the chain reaction in the reactor. Three seconds later, the reactor had suddenly heated up to half its capacity. The operators had no time to reinsert the rods. The emergency system couldn't turn off the reactor because it had been shut down. The coolant water inside the reactor instantly turned to steam because of the intense heat. The steam created an enormous amount of pressure that blew the 1,000-ton concrete top off. The radiation that escaped contaminated over a 1,000-square-mile area. The Soviet government estimates that between 6,500 to 40,000 of the people exposed will die from cancer.

The reactor at Chernobyl used a graphite moderator. The moderator in a nuclear reactor slows down the neutrons given off during fission. The graphite allowed the fission reaction to continue. In the United States, reactors use water as a moderator. If too little water reaches such a reactor, fission will stop.

In addition to the potential release of radiation during accidents, fission produces large amounts of nuclear waste. **Nuclear wastes** are the radioactive products of nuclear reactions. Many of the products of fission have long half-lives. Recall that half-life is the amount of time needed for one half of an amount of radioactive material to decay. To date, most radioactive wastes have been stored in tanks buried in the ground. Because the supplies of fossil fuels are decreasing, there may soon be an increase in the dependence upon nuclear energy. With such an increase would come an increase in the amount of radioactive wastes. How will people cope with these dangerous wastes? ■

On the line before each statement, write the letter of the choice that best completes the statement.

_____ 1. Advantages of nuclear reactors include _____.

    a. production of vast amounts of energy   c. the lack of air pollution

    b. the use of very little fuel   d. all of the above

_____ 2. In large doses, _____ are very dangerous to living organisms.

    a. alpha particles   b. cooling towers   c. gamma rays   d. moderators

_____ 3. In order to test the reactor at Chernobyl, workers _____.

    a. got the permission of supervisors   c. made sure that backup systems were left on

    b. left the control rods in place   d. none of the above

_____ 4. The accident at Chernobyl occurred within _____.

    a. a few seconds   b. several weeks   c. several hours   d. a month

_____ 5. The coolant water at the Chernobyl reactor turned to _____ during the test that caused the accident.

    a. graphite   b. steam   c. radioactive waste d. fission

_____ 6. It is estimated that _____ people exposed to radiation from the Chernobyl accident will die from _____.

    a. 65 to 400, heart attacks   c. 6,500 to 4,000, cancer

    b. 6,500 to 4,000, heart attacks   d. 6,500 to 40,000, cancer

_____ 7. _____ used as a moderator will stop fission in the event of a potential nuclear accident.

    a. Concrete   b. Graphite   c. Water   d. Waste

_____ 8. _____ are radioactive products of fission.

    a. Moderators   b. Reactors   c. Nuclear wastes   d. Control rods

● _____ 9. The nuclear accident at Chernobyl was due to _____.

    a. human errors   c. thermal pollution

    b. a water moderator   d. all of the above

● _____ 10. Underground storage tanks containing nuclear wastes pose potential problems because _____.

    a. they can be seen   c. the tanks can be reused

    b. radiation can penetrate soil   d. all of the above

Nuclear medicine technologists are trained in the proper use of the radioactive drugs that diagnose and treat various diseases.

Nuclear physicists conduct research in the field of nuclear energy. Most are employed by universities and other research institutions. Many are engaged in research in the area of nuclear fusion. Others specialize in the safe use and handling of radioactive materials. Some nuclear physicists are involved in the search for fuels that can be used in fission reactors. Nuclear physicists also serve as consultants to utility companies that operate nuclear power plants.

Nuclear engineers design, monitor, and operate the nuclear reactors used to generate electricity and to power nuclear vessels. They also conduct research on nuclear energy and radiation. Most nuclear engineers who conduct research are on the staffs of universities and research institutions. These scientists are working to make nuclear fusion a practical alternative to nuclear fission. A large number of nuclear engineers work for the federal government as civilian employees of the U.S. Navy and are involved in the nuclear submarine program. Some also work for the Department of Energy and for the Nuclear Regulatory Commission. Nuclear engineers may work for public utilities and for companies that provide engineering consulting services. Some work for companies that manufacture nuclear power equipment.

Nuclear medicine technologists are people who are trained in the proper use of radioactive drugs. They work directly with patients and administer radioactive substances that are given to diagnose and treat various diseases. The technologist observes the patient carefully to be sure there is no unanticipated reaction to the drug. These technologists also operate imaging equipment that is sensitive to the drugs and view the images on film or computer screens. Some nuclear medicine technologists work for drug companies. Many are employed by large hospitals and medical centers.

Nuclear technicians operate nuclear research and test equipment. Many are members of the staffs of research institutions. There, they assist nuclear engineers in various research studies. Some nuclear technicians work for companies that manufacture radioactive materials that are used in nuclear reactors. Other nuclear technicians work for power companies as members of the staffs that monitor the reactors at nuclear power plants.

Career opportunities exist for those with appropriate training in the field of nuclear energy. Those with a technical background can find positions in laboratories that conduct nuclear research. The nuclear power industry employs technicians who perform various tasks in power plant operation. Specialized jobs also exist in uranium mining and processing and in nuclear waste disposal. Nuclear medicine offers challenging opportunities for those who wish to undergo appropriate training. ■

For Further Information

More information about these and related careers is available from the following publications and oganizations.

Opportunities in Energy Careers, John Woodburn, VGM Career Horizons, 1979

Physics in Your Future, Dinah Moche, American Physical Society, 1982

American Nuclear Society
555 N. Kensington Avenue
La Grange Park, IL 60525

Atomic Industrial Forum
7101 Wisconsin Avenue
Washington, DC 20014

Society of Nuclear Medicine
475 Park Avenue South
New York, NY 10016

Glossary

The boldfaced numbers after each entry indicate the page on which the word is first defined.

acceleration (p. 6)—the increased rate of change of an object's velocity

acid rain (p. 81)—precipitation that carries sulfuric acid to Earth

acoustics (p. 64)—the science that studies sound

active solar-heating system (p. 26)—a heating system in which solar collectors absorb radiant energy from the sun and transfer this energy to water that they contain

air pollution (p. 81)—the introduction of harmful substances into the air

alpha particles (p. 86)—particles made up of two neutrons and two protons

alternating current (p. 34)—an electrical current in which electrons flow first in one direction and then in the opposite direction

amperage (p. 35)—the rate at which an electric current flows

amplifier (p. 38)—a transistor that builds a weak signal into a strong signal

angle of incidence (p. 46)—the angle at which light rays strike a smooth surface

angle of reflection (p. 46)—the angle at which light rays bounce off a surface

atomic number (p. 78)—the number of protons in the nucleus of an atom

atoms (p. 32)—the very tiny particles that make up all matter

beta particles (p. 86)—electrons that travel near the speed of light

block and tackle (p. 8)—a combination of two or more pulleys which can be used to lift heavy equipment

bubble chamber (p. 88)—a tightly sealed metal box with a viewing window that is used to detect radiation

cellular mobile telephone (p. 66)—a telephone that can make and receive calls from a moving vehicle

Celsius scale (p. 20)—a scale for measuring temperature in which water freezes at 0° and boils at 100°

central heating (p. 24)—a system in which one heat source is used to heat an entire house or building

chemical change (p. 73)—a change in a substance that makes it a new substance

chemical equation (p. 76)—an equation that represents the changes that occur during a chemical reaction

chemical formula (p. 75)—a group of symbols that represent a compound

circuit (p. 34)—the path followed by electrons from a source to an output device

cloud chamber (p. 88)—a container filled with supersaturated air that detects paths of electrically charged particles

coefficient (p. 76)—the number that serves to show the amount of a substance needed in a chemical equation

coherent light (p. 54)—light in which all the light waves travel in the same direction and have the same wavelengths

communications satellites (p. 67)—space-craft that orbit Earth with communications equipment to relay sound and visual messages from place to place

compound (p. 72)—a combination of different kinds of atoms in a certain ratio

compound machine (p. 9)—a machine made of two or more simple machines

compressional wave (p. 58)—a wave in which matter vibrates in the same direction as the wave travels

computer (p. 39)—an electronic device that solves complex problems by breaking them down into simpler problems

concave lens (p. 49)—a lens that is thinner in the middle than it is at the edges

concave mirror (p. 47)—a mirror that is curved like the bowl of a spoon

conduction (p. 22)—the transfer of thermal energy that takes place when two objects at different temperatures are in contact with one another

conductors (p. 22)—materials that transfer thermal energy

control rods (p. 92)—metal rods that regulate the speed of the chain reaction in a nuclear reactor

convection (p. 23)—the transfer of thermal energy by the actual movement of molecules

convex lens (p. 48)—a lens that is thicker in the middle than it is at the edges

convex mirror (p. 46)—a mirror that is curved like the back of a spoon

coolant (p. 92)—a gas or liquid that is used to remove thermal energy from a nuclear reactor

core (p. 92)—the central part of a nuclear reactor that contains the nuclear fuel

covalent bonds (p. 75)—bonds that form between elements when electrons are shared

current electricity (p. 33)—a continuous flow of electrons

dead spot (p. 64)—an area where hearing is very difficult or impossible

deceleration (p. 6)—the decreased rate of change in an object's velocity

decomposition (p. 77)—the processs in which a substance breaks down into one or more other substances

differential (p. 12)—a set of gears mounted at the center of a car's rear axle that transfers energy from the drive shaft to the drive wheels

diffraction (p. 52)—the bending of light waves that occurs when they pass through an opening or around the edges of an object

diffraction grating (p. 52)—a surface of numerous, very small, evenly spaced, parallel slits

direct current (p. 34)—an electrical current in which the electrons flow in only one direction

displacement reaction (p. 77)—a reaction in which one or more elements displace other elements from a compound

Doppler effect (p. 60)—effect that causes what appears to be a change in the pitch of a sound because of the motion of the source or the listener

drive shaft (p. 12)—a rod that runs from a car's transmission to the differential on the car's rear axle

dry cell (p. 34)—a type of battery that usually is made from chemical paste, a small carbon rod, and a zinc container

echoes (p. 64)—reflected sounds

efficiency (p. 10)—the relationship between the force a machine puts out and the force that it could put out without the forces of gravity, inertia, and friction acting upon it

effort (p. 8)—the force used to move an object

electric current (p. 34)—the flow of electrons or other charged particles through a conductor

electric motors (p. 36)—machines that change electrical energy into mechanical energy

electricity (p. 33)—energy caused by the transfer of electrons

electromagnet (p. 31)—a coil of wire which becomes a temporary magnet because of the electricity flowing through it

electromagnetic spectrum (p. 42)—the arrangement of electromagnetic waves according to their frequencies

electromagnetic waves (p. 42)—waves that do not have to travel through matter in order to transfer energy

electron (p. 32)—a subatomic particle with a negative $(-)$ electrical charge

element (p. 72)—matter that is made of only one kind of atom

energy (p. 4)—the ability to do work

Fahrenheit scale (p. 20)—a scale for measuring temperature in which water freezes at 32° and boils at 212°

feedback (p. 14)—the informational process that makes it possible to operate a machine, such as a robot, by computer

first law of motion (p. 6)—Newton's law that states that an object moving at a constant velocity will continue at that velocity unless acted upon by an outside force

fluorescence (p. 44)—luminescence, or light, that continues only while an outside source emits radiation

force (p. 5)—a push or pull that one body or object exerts on another

fossil fuels (p. 26)—fuels such as coal, oil, or natural gas that formed millions of years ago from the remains of plants and animals

frequency (p. 42)—the number of waves that pass a given point in one second

friction (p. 7)—a force that opposes or counteracts the motion between two surfaces that are in contact

fulcrum (p. 8)—a supporting point about which a lever turns

gamma rays (p. 43)—electromagnetic waves with small wavelengths and high frequency; forms of high energy radiation that have no electrical charges

gears (p. 12)—wheels with teeth, or notches, around their outer edges

Geiger counter (p. 88)—a device that detects radiation by the formation of an electric current

generators (p. 36)—machines that convert mechanical energy into electrical energy

gravity (p. 7)—a force that pulls objects toward Earth

group (p. 78)—a vertical column of elements in the periodic table that contains elements with similar properties

half-life (p. 87)—the amount of time that is needed for half of the atoms in a radioactive element to decay into another element

heat (p. 5)—the thermal energy that is transferred from an object at a higher temperature to an object at a lower temperature

heat pump (p. 25)—a heat mover that can both heat and cool a house or other building

inclined plane (p. 8)—a slanted surface

incoherent light (p. 54)—light in which the waves travel in different directions and have different wavelengths

inertia (p. 6)—the property of an object that resists any change in velocity

infrared waves (p. 43)—electromagnetic waves with wavelengths just a little longer than those of visible light

inorganic matter (p. 72)—any substance that is not living

input (p. 10)—the amount of energy that is put or designed into a machine

integrated circuit (p. 38)—a circuit that includes all of the rectifiers, amplifiers, oscillators, and other transistors needed to operate an electronic device

intensity (p. 59)—the amount of energy that is in a sound wave

interference (p. 52)—the ability of two or more waves to combine to form a new wave

ionic bonds (p. 75)—bonds that form between elements when elements transfer electrons

ions (p. 32)—atoms that have either gained or lost electrons

isotopes (p. 86)—forms of an element with different numbers of neutrons

kilowatt-hour (p. 35)—a measure of the thousands of watts of electricity used in one hour

kinetic energy (p. 4)—the energy of motion

larynx (p. 63)—the human voice box, which is located in the upper area of the trachea

laser (p. 54)—a device that produces an intense, narrow beam of light that is all one wavelength and one color

law of conservation of energy (p. 4)—scientific law that states that the amount of energy in the universe is always the same

lens (p. 48)—any curved, transparent material that refracts light waves

lever (p. 8)—a simple machine consisting of a rigid bar or rod that turns about a supporting point called a fulcrum

lightning (p. 33)—the electrical spark caused by the flow of electrons from a negatively-charged part of a cloud to an area with a positive charge

light-year (p. 45)—the distance that light travels in one year, which is equal to 186,000 miles per second

loudness (p. 59)—a person's response to the intensity of a sound

luminescence (p. 44)—the emission of visible light as the result of life, or biological, processes

luminous objects (p. 44)—objects that produce and emit their own light

machine (p. 8)—a device that does work by changing one form of energy into another form of energy in order to create force

magnetic field (p. 31)—the area around a magnet where objects are attracted or repelled

magnetic poles (p. 30)—the places on a magnet where the magnetic forces are strongest

magnetism (p. 30)—a property of some matter in which two objects are attracted, or pulled together, due to unlike poles

mass (p. 6)—the amount of matter that makes up an object

mass number (p. 86)—the number of protons and neutrons in the nucleus of an atom

matter (p. 32)—anything that takes up space and has mass

mechanical advantage (p. 10)—the number of times the effort is multiplied by using a machine to move the resistance

meltdown (p. 93)—a condition that takes place when the core of a nuclear reactor gets so hot that it "melts" or burns through the floor of the building that houses it

microchip (p. 38)—a silicon chip onto which all the transistors of an integrated circuit are pressed

microphone (p. 66)—a device that changes sound waves into electrical impulses

microprocessor (p. 39)—a single integrated circuit that can perform the mathematical calculations of a much larger computer

mixture (p. 72)—a kind of matter in which the parts composing it are combined in no certain ratios and each part keeps its own properties

moderator (p. 92)—a substance in a nuclear reactor, usually water, that slows down the neutrons formed during fission

motion (p. 6)—a change in position

neutron (p. 32)—a subatomic particle that has no electrical charge

noise (p. 62)—a sound with irregular vibrations

noise pollution (p. 68)—unwanted, disturbing, harmful, or annoying sounds

nonrenewable resources (p. 26)—materials from Earth that cannot be remade or replaced once they are used up

nuclear chain reaction (p. 90)—a continuous series of fission reactions

nuclear fission (p. 90)—a nuclear reaction that takes place when a heavy, radioactive nucleus splits to form two new nuclei

nuclear fusion (p. 91)—a reaction that occurs when two nuclei fuse, or combine, to form one heavier nucleus

nuclear reactor (p. 92)—a device that makes it possible to control the process of nuclear fission and to use the energy generated from the reaction

nuclear wastes (p. 94)—the radioactive products of nuclear reactions

nucleus (p. 32)—the center core of an atom where most of its mass, the protons and neutrons, is concentrated

opaque (p. 44)—materials through which light will not travel

organic matter (p. 72)—any substance that is alive or that came from a once-living organism

oscillator (p. 38)—a transistor that converts direct current into signals that operate on particular frequencies; a device that changes radio waves into electrical impulses

output (p. 10)—the work done by a machine

ozone layer (p. 81)—a layer of gas that protects Earth and its inhabitants from the harmful ultraviolet radiation from the sun

parallel circuit (p. 37)—an electrical circuit that provides two or more paths for a current to follow before it returns to its source

particulates (p. 81)—tiny pieces of solids that are added to the air when substances are burned

passive solar-heating system (p. 26)—a solar heating system in which energy is collected, distributed, and stored without using pumps

percussion instruments (p. 62)—musical instruments that produce sound as a result of being struck

period (p. 78)—a horizontal row of elements of the periodic table

periodic table (p. 78)—a scientific table that classifies the known elements according to their properties

permanent magnet (p. 31)—a magnet that keeps its magnetism

phosphorescence (p. 44)—luminescence that continues after the radiation of light stops

photons (p. 52)—the particles that make up light and all other forms of electromagnetic radiation

physical change (p. 73)—a change that does not change the chemical composition of matter

pitch (p. 60)—the way in which a listener hears the frequency of a sound

potential energy (p. 4)—energy that is stored and available for use

power (p. 10)—the rate at which a machine does work

pressure vessel (p. 92)—that part of a nuclear reactor that encases the core and contains channels through which coolant flows

prism (p. 50)—a transparent object that refracts, or bends, light rays into the colors of the visible spectrum

products (p. 76)—the substances on the right side of a chemical equation

proton (p. 32)—a subatomic particle with a positive (+) electrical charge

pulley (p. 8)—a simple machine in which a rope or cable is strung over a grooved wheel

quality (p. 60)—the characteristic of sound that allows a listener to identify it with a certain source

radiation (p.23)—the transfer of thermal energy that can take place in a vacuum.

radioactive decay (p. 86)—the process during which charged particles, or radiation, are given off

radio waves (p. 42)—electromagnetic waves with the longest wavelengths

reactants (p. 78)—the substances on the left side of a chemical equation

rectifier (p. 38)—a transistor that changes alternating current into direct current

reflection (p. 46)—the process by which light strikes an object and bounces off it

refraction (p. 48)—the bending of light rays that occurs when light passes through certain materials

resistance (p. 8, 36)—the weight of an object being moved by a machine; an opposing force similar to friction in an electrical circuit

reverberation (p. 64)—sound made up of many echoes traveling so close together that no one echo can be heard

robot (p. 14)—a machine that usually remains in a fixed position and is guided by a computer to complete a task

robotics (p. 14)—the science and technology of designing and using robots to do work

safety shields (p. 93)—shields the total energy, both kinetic and potential, of all the molecules that make up a substance

screw (p. 9)—an inclined plane wrapped around a shaft or cylinder

second law of motion (p. 7)—Newton's law that states that the acceleration of an object increases as the amount of force applied on the object increases

sensor (p. 14)—an electronic device that transmits information about a robot's performance and surroundings to a computer

series circuit (p. 37)—an electrical circuit that provides a single path along which electricity flows to the objects that use it

smog (p. 81)—a kind of air pollution that forms when a chemical reaction occurs among sunlight, nitric oxide, carbon dioxide, sulfur dioxide, and compounds containing carbon and hydrogen

solar collectors (p. 26)—devices that collect the sun's radiant energy

solution (p. 73)—a mixture in which the components are evenly distributed and cannot be easily separated

speed (p. 6)—the rate of change of the position of an object

static electricity (p. 33)—the electrical charge that is built up in one place

stimulated emission (p. 54)—a process in which excited atoms give off light systematically

stringed instruments (p. 62)—musical instruments that produce sounds because at least one string vibrates as the result of being plucked or moved with a bow

supersaturated air (p. 88)—air that contains more water vapor than usual at a given temperature

symbol (p. 74)—an abbreviation of one, two, or three letters that stand for an element of the periodic table

synthesis (p. 77)—the reaction that occurs when two or more elements or compounds join to form one new compound

telegraph (p. 66)—a device that uses a complete electrical circuit to send messages over great distances

temperature (p. 18)—a measure of the average kinetic energy of the molecules that make up an object

temporary magnet (p. 31)—a magnet that loses its magnetism

thermal energy (p. 18)—the total energy, both kinetic and potential, of all the molecules that make up a substance

thermal pollution (p. 81)—a form of water pollution caused when factories or power plants discharge heated water into local bodies of water

thermometer (p. 20)—an instrument, partially filled with mercury or colored alcohol, that is used for measuring temperature

thermostat (p. 25)—a device that automatically responds to temperature changes and activates switches to control a furnace

third law of motion (p. 7)—Newton's law that states that forces always come in pairs, and that for every action, there is an opposite and equal reaction

tracers (p. 88)—radioactive isotopes that can be used to follow a mechanical or biological process

trachea (p. 63)—a tube that carries air to the human lungs

transformers (p. 37)—electrical devices that increase or decrease voltage used in an electrical-transport system

transistor (p. 38)—a part of an electronic device that changes electrical current into signals

translucent (p. 44)—materials that allow some light to pass through them

transparent (p. 45)—materials that allow light to travel completely through them

transverse wave (p. 58)—a wave in which matter moves at right angles to the direction the wave travels

ultrasounds (p. 61)—sounds with frequencies higher than 20,000 hertz

ultraviolet light (p. 43)—light with a shorter wavelength than visible light

velocity (p. 6)—an object's speed and the direction in which it is moving

voltage (p. 34)—the potential difference between the electrons at the negative terminal and the electrons at the positive terminal of a battery

wattage (p. 35)—electrical power; the voltage multiplied by the amperage

wave (p. 42)—a rhythmic disturbance that carries energy

wavelength (p. 42)—the distance from the trough of one wave to the trough of the next wave, or from the crest of one wave to the crest of the next wave

wedge (p. 8)—an inclined plane that has either one or two slanted edges

weight (p. 7)—the force of gravity that Earth exerts on an object at its surface

wet cell (p. 34)—a type of battery that consists of two metal plates in an acidic solution

wheel and axle (p. 8)—a simple machine that consists of a large wheel that is attached to a smaller wheel or rod called an axle

white light (p. 50)—a mixture of all of the colors of the visible spectrum; ordinary sunlight

wind instruments (p. 62)—musical instruments whose sounds are produced by columns of air that vibrate within the instruments

work (p. 4)—the transfer of energy as the result of motion

X rays (p. 43)—radiant energy with wavelengths shorter than the wavelengths of ultraviolet light

This Mastery Review is an opportunity to check your understanding of the content of this book. Part 1 measures the first four units, and Part 2 measures the last three units.

This Mastery Review should take no longer than one hour to complete. If you come to questions that you cannot answer, move on. When you have answered the questions that you know, try those that you skipped. To record your answers, fill in the numbered space on your answer sheet that matches the number of the correct answer.

Part 1 (Sections A, B, and C cover material in Units 1–4.)

A. In Questions 1–18, a phrase is followed by four terms. Mark the term that the phrase best defines or identifies.

1. a device that transmits information about a robot's surroundings to a computer
   (1) thermometer   (2) sensor   (3) differential   (4) wedge

2. anything that occupies space and has mass
   (1) energy   (2) power   (3) current   (4) matter

3. devices that reduce the amount of energy needed to move heavy objects
   (1) atoms   (2) machines   (3) lenses   (4) angles

4. instrument that measures temperature
   (1) thermometer   (2) oscillator   (3) wet cell   (4) antenna

5. the transfer of energy as a result of motion
   (1) heat   (2) current   (3) work   (4) power

6 force that pulls objects toward Earth
   (1) gravity   (2) inertia   (3) velocity   (4) friction

7. a continuous flow of electrons
   (1) neutrons   (2) ions   (3) neurons   (4) current electricity

8. occurs when light strikes an object and bounces off it
   (1) radiation   (2) reflection   (3) refraction   (4) static electricity

9. a rhythmic disturbance that carries energy
   (1) spectrum   (2) frequency   (3) prism   (4) wave

10. an inclined plane wrapped around a cylinder
   (1) wedge   (2) screw   (3) pulley   (4) fulcrum

11. the ability to do work
    (1) power   (2) force   (3) energy   (4) effort

12. the particles from which visible light is made
    (1) photons   (2) atoms   (3) molecules   (4) waves

13. a push or pull that one body exerts upon another
    (1) force   (2) effort   (3) power   (4) energy

14. the opposition to the flow of electrical current
    (1) voltage   (2) circuit   (3) power   (4) resistance

15. device that increases and decreases voltage
    (1) generator   (2) transformer   (3) circuit   (4) transistor

16. example of static electricity
    (1) lamp   (2) lightning   (3) rainbow   (4) alternating current

17. the relationship between the force a machine is capable of putting out and its actual output
    (1) advantage   (2) effort   (3) resistance   (4) efficiency

18. the transfer of thermal energy by an actual movement of molecules
    (1) convection   (2) radiation   (3) conduction   (4) effort

B. Questions 19–35 each contain a blank space and are followed by four choices. Mark the word or phrase that best completes each statement.

19. _____ energy is found in gasoline and in other fuels.
    (1) Mechanical   (2) Radiant   (3) Electrical   (4) Chemical

20. The _____ is the rate at which an electric current flows.
    (1) radiation   (2) wattage   (3) amperage   (4) circuit

21. Materials that transfer thermal energy are called _____.
    (1) conductors   (2) resistors   (3) amplifiers   (4) capacitors

22. The _____ are the places on a magnet that have the strongest magnetic force.
    (1) points   (2) fields   (3) cells   (4) poles

23. The mass of an atom is concentrated in its _____.
    (1) ions   (2) fields   (3) nucleus   (4) orbit

24. _____ rays have a very short wavelength and can penetrate almost any kind of material.
    (1) Gamma   (2) Radio   (3) Ultraviolet   (4) Infrared

25. A(n) _____ is a subatomic particle with a positive electric charge.
    (1) neutron   (2) proton   (3) ion   (4) electron

26. _____ refers to an object's speed and the direction in which it is moving.
    (1) Motion   (2) Velocity   (3) Acceleration   (4) Inertia

27. The force of _____ opposes motion between two surfaces that are in contact.
    (1) gravity   (2) inertia   (3) friction   (4) weight

28. _____ is the bending of light rays that occurs when light passes through water.
    (1) Absorption   (2) Refraction   (3) Interference   (4) Reflection

29. Atoms that have either gained or lost electrons are called _____.
    (1) ions   (2) neutrons   (3) molecules   (4) protons

30. An object's _____ is the force of gravity that pulls it toward Earth.
    (1) mass   (2) weight   (3) power   (4) speed

31. A(n) _____ is a slanted surface.
    (1) pulley   (2) lever   (3) wheel and axle   (4) inclined plane

32. A(n) _____ is a device that controls a furnace by responding to temperature changes.
    (1) amplifier   (2) thermometer   (3) valve   (4) thermostat

33. Light bulbs change electrical energy into thermal energy and _____ energy.
    (1) chemical   (2) radiant   (3) mechanical   (4) magnetic

34. Light will not travel through _____ materials.
    (1) opaque   (2) luminescent   (3) transparent   (4) translucent

35. A _____ mirror is curved like the bowl of a spoon.
    (1) convex   (2) fluorescent   (3) concave   (4) luminous

C. **In each pair of statements in questions 36–42, one is true and the other is false. Mark the statement that is true.**

36. (1) An electromagnet is a permanent magnet.
    (2) If the flow of electricity stops, an electromagnet loses its magnetism.

37. (1) The law of conservation of energy states that energy cannot be created or destroyed.
    (2) The law of conservation of energy states that energy can be created and destroyed.

38. (1) Heat moves from an object at a higher temperature to an object at a lower temperature.
    (2) Heat moves from an object at a lower temperature to an object at a higher temperature.

39. (1) A machine's input is the energy that it releases.
    (2) A machine's output is the energy that it releases.

40. (1) An object with a large mass has more thermal energy than an object with a small mass.
    (2) An object with a large mass has less thermal energy than an object with a small mass.

41. (1) If a permanent magnet is broken in half, it will lose its magnetism.
    (2) If a permanent magnet is broken in half, each half will keep its magnetism.

42. (1) The moon is a luminous object.
    (2) Stars are luminous objects.

Part 2 (Sections D, E, and F cover material in Units 5–7.)

D. In questions 43–52, a phrase is followed by four terms. Mark the term that the phrase best defines or identifies. Fill in the circle on the answer sheet whose number corresponds with your choice.

43. device that uses a complete electrical circuit to send messages over great distances
    (1) telegraph
    (2) communications satellite
    (3) percussion instrument
    (4) pitch

44. matter that is made of only one kind of atom
    (1) mixture
    (2) element
    (3) solution
    (4) compound

45. group of symbols that represent a compound
    (1) ionic bond
    (2) oxidation
    (3) chemical formula
    (4) frequency

46. what every sound wave is caused by
    (1) frequency
    (2) pitch
    (3) noise
    (4) vibration

47. musical wind instrument
    (1) tuba
    (2) violin
    (3) drum
    (4) piano

48. number of protons in atom's nucleus
    (1) group number
    (2) atomic number
    (3) period number
    (4) member number

49. chemical reaction in which two or more elements or compounds are joined
    (1) displacement
    (2) decomposition
    (3) solution
    (4) synthesis

50. gas layer that protects Earth from the sun's ultraviolet rays
    (1) ozone
    (2) hydrogen
    (3) environmental
    (4) particulate

51. different forms of an element
    (1) solutions
    (2) products
    (3) isotopes
    (4) neutrons

52. a reaction that takes place when heavy, radioactive nuclei split to form two new nuclei
    (1) nuclear energy
    (2) meltdown
    (3) nuclear fusion
    (4) nuclear fission

E. Questions 53–67 each contain a blank space and are followed by four choices. Mark the word or phrase that best completes each statement.

53. During a(n) _____ change, a substance becomes a new substance.
    (1) sound
    (2) physical
    (3) chemical
    (4) light

54. _____ is the way in which a person hears the frequency of a sound.
    (1) Quality
    (2) Loudness
    (3) Hertz
    (4) Pitch

55. The result of the many reflections of sound waves is called _____.
    (1) reverberation
    (2) acoustics
    (3) frequency
    (4) absorption

56. Currently, there are _____ known elements.
    (1) 18
    (2) 109
    (3) 106
    (4) 118

57. Light travels _____.
   (1) in a straight line   (2) through rock   (3) around corners   (4) 186 miles a year

58. Radiation that penetrates matter most deeply is _____.
   (1) gamma rays   (2) molecules   (3) beta particles   (4) alpha particles

59. The _____ are elements that do not easily combine with other elements.
   (1) oxygen group   (2) noble gases   (3) boron group   (4) transition group

60. Scientists use _____ to represent how elements react in the presence of other elements.
   (1) chemical equations   (2) a periodic table   (3) atomic numbers   (4) products

61. When substances are burned, tiny pieces of solids called _____ pollute the air.
   (1) particulates   (2) reactants   (3) protons   (4) thermals

62. Radioactive isotopes called _____ are used to follow a mechanical or biological process.
   (1) neutrons   (2) neurons   (3) tracers   (4) solutions

63. When unstable atoms _____, tremendous amounts of energy are released.
   (1) decay   (2) explode   (3) collide   (4) heat up

64. In nuclear _____, two nuclei combine to form a heavier nucleus.
   (1) reactors   (2) fissions   (3) chain reactions   (4) fusion

65. Without a _____, the chain reaction in a nuclear reactor might not occur.
   (1) moderator   (2) pressure vessel   (3) safety system   (4) coolant

66. The nuclear accident at Chernobyl happened because of _____.
   (1) design problems   (2) weather   (3) material breakdown   (4) human error

67. _____ is an example of inorganic matter.
   (1) Wheat   (2) Rice   (3) Iron   (4) Cotton

F. **In each pair of statements below, one is true and the other is false. Mark the statement that is true. Fill in the circle on the answer sheet whose number corresponds with your choice.**

68. (1) Light travels faster than sound.
    (2) Sound travels faster than light.

69. (1) A microphone changes sound waves into light waves.
    (2) A microphone changes sound waves into electrical impulses.

70. (1) Sound waves are transverse waves produced by vibrating matter.
    (2) Sound waves are compressional waves produced by vibrating matter.

Name _____

Mastery Review Answer Sheet

TEST ANSWERS

Fill in the circle corresponding to your answer for each question. Erase cleanly.

Part 1

A

1 ① ② ③ ④
2 ① ② ③ ④
3 ① ② ③ ④
4 ① ② ③ ④
5 ① ② ③ ④
6 ① ② ③ ④
7 ① ② ③ ④
8 ① ② ③ ④
9 ① ② ③ ④
10 ① ② ③ ④
11 ① ② ③ ④
12 ① ② ③ ④
13 ① ② ③ ④
14 ① ② ③ ④
15 ① ② ③ ④
16 ① ② ③ ④
17 ① ② ③ ④
18 ① ② ③ ④

B

19 ① ② ③ ④
20 ① ② ③ ④
21 ① ② ③ ④
22 ① ② ③ ④
23 ① ② ③ ④
24 ① ② ③ ④
25 ① ② ③ ④
26 ① ② ③ ④
27 ① ② ③ ④
28 ① ② ③ ④
29 ① ② ③ ④
30 ① ② ③ ④
31 ① ② ③ ④
32 ① ② ③ ④
33 ① ② ③ ④
34 ① ② ③ ④
35 ① ② ③ ④

C

36 ① ② ③ ④
37 ① ② ③ ④
38 ① ② ③ ④
39 ① ② ③ ④
40 ① ② ③ ④
41 ① ② ③ ④
42 ① ② ③ ④

Part 2

D

43 ① ② ③ ④
44 ① ② ③ ④
45 ① ② ③ ④
46 ① ② ③ ④
47 ① ② ③ ④
48 ① ② ③ ④
49 ① ② ③ ④
50 ① ② ③ ④
51 ① ② ③ ④
52 ① ② ③ ④

E

53 ① ② ③ ④
54 ① ② ③ ④
55 ① ② ③ ④
56 ① ② ③ ④
57 ① ② ③ ④
58 ① ② ③ ④
59 ① ② ③ ④
60 ① ② ③ ④
61 ① ② ③ ④
62 ① ② ③ ④
63 ① ② ③ ④
64 ① ② ③ ④
65 ① ② ③ ④
66 ① ② ③ ④
67 ① ② ③ ④

F

68 ① ② ③ ④
69 ① ② ③ ④
70 ① ② ③ ④

Answer Key

Unit 1

Lesson 1	Lesson 2	Lesson 3	Lesson 4	Lesson 5	Issues in Science
1. b	1. Motion	1. c	1. inertia, gravity	1. b	1. computer
2. c	2. speed	2. g	2. Mechanical advantage	2. e	2. Robotics
3. d	3. first	3. b	3. less	3. h	3. difficult
4. b	4. Inertia	4. f	4. output	4. d	4. Feedback
5. c	5. mass	5. j	5. Efficiency	5. c	5. welding
6. a	6. less	6. h	6. low	6. j	6. sensors
7. b	7. pairs	7. a	7. friction	7. f	7. hazardous
8. d	8. more	8. i	8. power	8. i	8. adjustments
9. d	9. velocity	9. d	9. six	9. a	9. microchips
10. d	10. decreases	10. e	10. high	10. g	10. visual

Unit 2

Lesson 1	Lesson 2	Lesson 3	Lesson 4	Issues in Science
1. c	1. c	1. T	1. open fireplaces	1. F *(fossil fuels for the sun)*
2. a	2. a	2. F *(Conduction for Convection)*	2. conduction, convection, radiation	2. T
3. c	3. c	3. F *(an increase for a decrease)*	3. less	3. F *(cannot for can)*
4. b	4. b	4. T	4. Central heating	4. T
5. d	5. c	5. T	5. metal jacket	5. F *(radiant for kinetic)*
6. d	6. b	6. F *(more for less)*	6. thermostat	6. F *(an active for a passive)*
7. c	7. b	7. T	7. heat mover	7. F *(a passive for an active)*
8. b	8. c	8. F *(Radiation for Convection)*	8. removes	8. F *(can for cannot)*
9. d	9. b	9. T	9. remove	9. F *(less for more)*
10. b	10. c	10. F *(floor for ceiling)*	10. convection	10. F *(less for more)*

Unit 3

Lesson 1	Lesson 2	Lesson 3	Lesson 4	Issues in Science
1. e	1. Electricity	1. c	1. electrical	1. c
2. d	2. matter	2. a	2. resistance	2. j
3. f	3. proton	3. d	3. length, thickness	3. i
4. b	4. protons	4. b	4. resistance	4. a
5. j	5. positively	5. c	5. radiant, thermal	5. d
6. c	6. electrons, wool, comb	6. a	6. Electric motors	6. e
7. g	7. static	7. a	7. Generators	7. b
8. a	8. Current	8. c	8. parallel	8. f
9. i	9. positive	9. c	9. more	9. h
10. h	10. negative	10. b	10. 27	10. g

Unit 4

Lesson 1
1. b
2. c
3. d
4. d
5. a
6. b
7. a
8. d
9. c
10. b

Lesson 2
1. a
2. d
3. d
4. c
5. a
6. d
7. a
8. b
9. a
10. a

Lesson 3
1. T
2. F *(upright for upside down)*
3. F *(incidence for reflection)*
4. F *(smooth for rough)*
5. T
6. F *(smaller for larger)*
7. T
8. T
9. F *(are not able for are able)*
10. T

Lesson 4
1. d
2. c
3. d
4. a
5. a
6. c
7. b
8. b
9. c
10. b

Lesson 5
1. White light
2. prism
3. red, orange, blue, violet
4. drops of water
5. reflected
6. all
7. absorbs
8. Colorblindness
9. red-green
10. green, black

Lesson 6
1. c
2. d
3. a
4. b
5. a
6. d
7. b
8. c
9. c
10. d

Issues in Science
1. F *(one wavelength and color for wavelengths and colors)*
2. T
3. F *(incoherent for coherent)*
4. T
5. T
6. F *(a red for an invisible)*
7. F *(high for low)*
8. T
9. F *(decrease for increase)*
10. T

Unit 5

Lesson 1
1. j
2. a
3. b
4. c
5. f
6. d
7. e
8. i
9. g
10. h

Lesson 2
1. T
2. F *(and pitch for only)*
3. F *(Pitch for Loudness)*
4. T
5. T
6. F *(Doppler for Ultrasound)*
7. F *(cannot for can)*
8. T
9. T
10. T

Lesson 3
1. quality, loudness
2. noise
3. music
4. noise
5. Percussion
6. wind
7. stringed
8. vocal cords
9. higher
10. wind

Lesson 4
1. c
2. d
3. d
4. c
5. d
6. b
7. d
8. a
9. b
10. c

Lesson 5
1. telegraph
2. dots
3. teletype
4. receiver
5. microphone
6. antenna
7. computer
8. Fiber optics
9. communications
10. faster

Issues in Science
1. T
2. T
3. T
4. F *(more than for less than)*
5. T
6. F *(hard for easy)*
7. F *(120-130 for 20)*
8. T
9. T
10. F *(less for more)*

Unit 6

Lesson 1	Lesson 2	Lesson 3		Lesson 4	Issues in Science
1. particles	1. c	1. T		1. Mendeleev	1. d
2. Organic matter	2. a	2. F	$(C_6$ for $C_7)$	2. properties	2. a
3. solid	3. c	3. F	(equation for formula)	3. group	3. d
4. elements	4. c	4. T		4. period	4. b
5. mixture	5. b	5. F	(the same for different)	5. atomic number	5. c
6. solution	6. c	6. F	(four for two)	6. transition	6. d
7. physical	7. a	7. T		7. boron	7. a
8. chemical	8. c	8. T		8. fertilizers	8. d
9. mixture	9. a	9. T		9. transition, fifth	9. b
10. compound	10. c	10. T		10. 36	10. d

Unit 7

Lesson 1	Lesson 2		Lesson 3	Lesson 4	Issues in Science
1. b	1. F	(cannot for can)	1. h	1. nuclear reactor	1. d
2. c	2. T		2. e	2. electricity	2. c
3. a	3. F	(cloud for bubble)	3. g	3. core	3. d
4. a	4. T		4. b	4. moderator	4. a
5. c	5. T		5. d	5. control rods	5. b
6. b	6. T		6. c	6. water	6. d
7. d	7. T		7. a	7. pressure vessel	7. c
8. c	8. F	(electrons for protons)	8. f	8. Meltdown	8. c
9. a	9. F	(Tracers for Geiger	9. j	9. radiation	9. a
10. d		counters)	10. i	10. inserted	10. b
	10. T				

Mastery Review
Answer Key

Part 1

A

1. 2	7. 4	13. 1
2. 4	8. 2	14. 4
3. 2	9. 4	15. 2
4. 1	10. 2	16. 2
5. 3	11. 3	17. 4
6. 1	12. 1	18. 1

B

19. 4	25. 2	31. 4
20. 3	26. 2	32. 4
21. 1	27. 3	33. 2
22. 4	28. 2	34. 1
23. 3	29. 1	35. 3
24. 1	30. 2	

C

36. 2
37. 1
38. 1
39. 2
40. 1
41. 2
42. 2

Part 2

D

43. 1	48. 2
44. 2	49. 4
45. 3	50. 1
46. 4	51. 3
47. 1	52. 4

E

53. 3	56. 2	60. 1	64. 4
54. 2	57. 1	61. 1	65. 1
55. 1	58. 1	62. 3	66. 4
	59. 2	63. 1	67. 3

F

68. 1
69. 2
70. 2